I0460171

When the Bedbugs Bite
A Memoir of My Queer Life

Daniel Kelty

Copyright © 2025 by Daniel Kelty
All rights reserved.

No part of this publication may be reproduced, stored in a retrieval system, or
transmitted in any form or by any means—electronic, mechanical, photocopying,
recording, or otherwise—without the prior written permission of the copyright
owner, except for brief quotations used in reviews, scholarly works, or articles.

When the Bedbugs Bite
ISBN: 979-8-9990275-0-4

Edited by Rowan Kelty
Published by Pride Quill Publishing
415 Lake Vista Dr., Zanesville, OH 43701
614-370-1033 | pridequillpublishing.com

This is a work of nonfiction. Some names and identifying details may have been
changed to protect individuals' privacy.

Content Warning:
This memoir contains descriptions of suicide, child abuse, addiction, and other
traumatic experiences. Reader discretion is advised.

For more information about the author, visit danielkelty.com
Printed in the United States of America
First Edition

This book is dedicated to:
My sweet Lily,
My brave Jon
&
My strong Timothy

Introduction

In this book I often refer to myself as queer. For those not a part of the LGBTQIA community, I'd like to provide a moment of clarification here. For some readers, this word may induce a cringeworthy moment. That's good. That means you understand the historical context. The acronym LGBTQ, or alphabet soup, as I call it, that is currently used just feels too much for me. When I use the word queer to refer to people in my community, my intention is the respectful inclusion of people who identify as: gay, lesbian, bisexual, transgender, questioning and non-conforming gender expressions. Did I miss anyone? See why I use queer?

If any word can pick up a negative meaning or a derogatory meaning, it will eventually drive out all the positive ones if there is no push back, especially if that term is applied to underserved communities. It happens constantly in the evolution of language and tends to change as our vocabulary and our cultures change and grow but particularly with words that place people into minority groups.

Historically, the term once meant unusual but started to change around the 1500s to mean "dubious" or "not that great". Sometime afterwards, queer started being used as an insult directed at LGBTQ people. Some sources indicate people began reappropriating queer after the Stonewall riots in 1969. A more neutral or positive definition did not start cementing itself until the 1990s. One of the earliest representations cited by the Oxford English Dictionary is a newspaper report about a woman at a march in 1987 holding a placard, "We're Here Because We're Queer". Advocacy groups, like Queer Nation in New York City and Queer Action in Victoria, started adopting the term from the 1990s to represent "diversity of sexuality and diversity of our political focus".

For whatever reason, people need categories. We need boxes. We now know, we also need to break free from those boxes and be able to express our true selves. It helps us understand and identify. The problem arises when those boxes become restrictive because they serve to protect us from one another, to fear one another. The travesty is that this whole time we could have been learning from each other.

I will tell you that I identify as queer, because gay no longer fits, or never has fit, my self-definition. The word gay is tied into a specific cross-section of culture and community. I found myself in a place where that word no longer fit. It was too limiting.

It has been empowering for me to take ownership of the term queer because in my childhood, it instilled fear. It represented violence and elimination. It described freaks of nature. So, for me, the idea of reclaiming it, took away the power.

I remember first hearing the word used casually in homophobic jokes told by my uncles and cousins. I must have been about 12 years old when I heard my uncle boast, "Hey, ya know what they do with foreskin from babies after they are circumcised? They use it for bubble gum for queers!" The laughter ensued, and I shrunk back into the shadows, terrified of who I was and convinced I was going to burn in hell.

I remember being so shocked at the casual, ignorant dehumanization.

The danger is, of course, when you can remove someone's humanity, it is much easier to cause them harm. They become othered. The Midwest, and Ohio specifically, has always been a place where gay violence is common. It's a real risk and often determines how out we choose to be based on our support system.

Years ago, I remember hearing Matthew Sheppard's mom speak at Wright State University in Dayton, Ohio.

If you don't know, Matthew Shepard was a young gay man whose brutal murder in October 1998 became a pivotal moment in the fight against anti-LGBTQ hate crimes in the United States. He was a 21-year-old college student at the University of Wyoming, known for his gentle nature and passion for equality. On the night of October 6, 1998, Matthew was lured from a bar by two men who targeted him because of his sexual orientation. He was beaten, tortured, and left tied to a fence in a remote area near Laramie, Wyoming, where he was discovered 18 hours later by a passing cyclist. Matthew succumbed to his injuries on October 12, 1998. His death galvanized national and international outrage, ultimately leading to the passage of the Matthew Shepard and James Byrd, Jr. Hate Crimes Prevention Act in 2009.

Sitting in that audience, her words echoed in my ear and sat there in my head as my brain tried to imagine, tried to make sense of it. I was sitting about 10 rows back from the stage, but I could see her tears that ran down her face as she spoke. Each tremor in her voice carried the weight of unbearable pain, etching her grief into the room. I was humbled, almost reverent. Then I realized, 'my god. She must relive this each time she tells the story.' In that realization, part of me wanted her to stop talking. "Stop. Stop saying the words", I thought. "You don't have to do this."

But the reality was that she did have to do it. It was cathartic for her to be heard, to help others understand. The fact that just listening to the story was like running a razor-sharp knife across a scabbed-over wound just tells you the depth of her trauma.

No human being should ever have to experience that. This savage inhumane behavior of tying someone to a fucking fence and brutally beating them to death. That all comes from fear; fear that is based on words used to make us feel afraid, shameful and immoral.

Fundamentalist and conservatives will have you believe that the savage immoral people of the world are those of us who are queer, the Matthew Sheppards of the world. They are wrong.

The savage immoral people all start off being the innocent little boys and girls. Boys and girls who at some time were someone's sweet, precious child are taught to hate, fear, destroy, and kill. All this started with words. After the words came fear, and after that came action. If we challenge the words, we address the fear and change the action.

We can undo this if we learn to see one another's humanity. Till then, I will speak my truth without apology.

In my life, I've stepped back into the closet on some level at different times and not always by my own choice but to make other people comfortable. I'm done making other people's comfort my priority. If any part of this makes you uncomfortable, pay attention to that feeling and ask yourself, "Why?" Explore this discomfort. That's how we change it.

I have met many people who, after having heard some of my life stories, say, "Oh my god, you should write a book!" Well, here you go. I have sat down several times in my life and started this. I have at least fifteen or twenty different beginnings

I have written out of anger and stopped because I calmed down.

I have written out of pride and stopped because I felt ashamed.

I have written out of boredom and stopped because I got busy.

Queer culture is being erased. It's being ignored. It should be a part of history and sociology curricula taught in schools, but it's not. Even worse, there always seems to be some lingering legislation to outlaw us, our rights, and sometimes even our existence, because where there is no education, toxic religious rhetoric fills that gap.

If we don't step up and speak our truth, queer people in generations to come will likely experience continued devastation and violence. Today, I write for myself. I write for you. I write to document for queer people after me, to encourage, to educate and to never let the story stop with me.

Obviously, I have not written about every event and detail in my life. The stories that I feel have added weight to my journey, the ones that I feel carried a message of some sort, that's what I've included here.

Letter to my 10-year-old self

Hey Buddy…

I know things were scary sometimes. You were trying so hard to be good, to be enough, to be unnoticed when you needed, and to be un-forgettable when you wanted to be.

And no one told you back then that your softness was strength. That your glitter was gold. That your heartbreak would become a map one day — not just for you, but for others.

But here's the truth:

You grew up to be a man who's still here, who tells the truth even when his voice shakes, who left toxic love and still believes in family, and who loves his children with a kind of power that breaks cycles wide open.

You built a life from broken bricks, turned pain into purpose, and are literally helping people flourish after being rejected for who they are. You became the kind of man you never saw growing up.

And you know what else?
You're not done yet.

Chapter One
Zanesville

My intention for writing this book is to share my journey. It's a collection of thoughts, coping strategies, and stories. I have found them helpful in my career and personal life. I carry them around like special little rocks I've picked up on a walk. I don't know what purpose they serve. They don't take up nearly as much space as they used to. There was a time when these little rocks were boulders that not only could I not carry but that kept me trapped and isolated as I crouched behind them. Within their coldness and unyielding power, I found desperation and hopelessness.

The stories I am sharing in this book used to define me. They were, in my mind, bad things that happened to me because of some poor choice I had made. I no longer believe that. I share them with you because that's what turns those boulders into a handful of small pebbles. They no longer control me, define me, nor do they dictate my value. I had to find all those things on my own.

These stories are what I experienced. I am aware that I am certainly not the first queer man to have these things happen, but they happened to me and this is the story of how I experienced them. We all seek healing in different ways. This is mine.

I'm an openly queer man living in a small town as I write this. My two adopted sons are African-American in a predominantly white community. When my oldest son was in middle school, he described the experience as being "a black dot in the room of white people." I'm also an atheist in a Christian-dominated community as well as a liberal, cannabis using socialist in a red sea of republicans, so there's that little gem.

As I write this, my family lives in Zanesville, Ohio, though none of us are from there. It's just where we landed for several reasons that are explained later in this book. With few exceptions, the midwestern Appalachian folk here in Zanesville are, without question, nice—but they are often not kind. It's important not to confuse one with the other. Niceness and kindness are not the same. We've encountered little overt homophobia in this area. My boys have endured some instances of racism in school, but even that has been more passive and ignorant rather than aggressive.

No one is burning crosses on our lawn, breaking our windows, or shouting hateful slurs. That is how they show their niceness—a surface-level civility that avoids open hostility.

Even the people we've befriended here often keep us at arm's length. Social invitations rarely come our way—no dinners, no shared outings with other families. There are invisible yet rigid boundaries drawn around social circles, and if you don't meet certain unspoken criteria, no amount of niceness will result in being included. I've seen it firsthand.

We've invited countless kids and families to our children's birthday parties over the years, only to find ourselves scrambling to manage the awkwardness when one or two children show up—or, sometimes, none at all. In these moments, the veneer of niceness dissolves, revealing a lack of true kindness. People may smile politely and offer their apologies for not being able to make it, but the truth is often clearer than their words. I once had a parent say, with unsettling honesty, "Yeah, we got your party invitation. Thank you! We didn't come because we don't know you."

Nice versus kind; it's a distinction that matters. And here, it makes all the difference.

Even the most rural of communities is going to have, at the very least, a façade of a gay community. Zanesville is certainly no exception to that rule. Woven tightly within the simple-minded nature of Zanesville communities, there are pockets of seemingly liberal culture. Rainbow flags and liberal posters serve as a contrast to the sea of rebel flags and conservative religious propaganda. It gives the illusion of diversity, but it's not real; it's just less ugly.

Zanesville is home to not one but two community theater organizations, for example. While this duality was, at first, a surprising source of hope, I have surmised that this duality was not so much a reflection of growth of culture or social awareness but rather a result of two tiny social groups both determined to be the big fish in a small pond. Due to local popularity contests, the primary theater split into two. Both organizations drew their loyal community thespians.

It's rather like divorced parents that get along well. Everyone is polite, but the whispers of gossip and loyalty to social cliques were palpable. Both organizations largely function by supporting one another by scheduling back-to-back shows to stay afloat and sharing casts and crews. However, there was an undying incestuous gatekeeping that not only prohibits growth but suffocates any outside influences so that internal egos can thrive.

I love theater, but I found the culture here to be just like a toxic dysfunctional family, so I had little tolerance for it, unfortunately. The performances were fun, and some of the kids were great but after a couple years of back-to-back Disney shows, it became clear I had stepped into a high school popularity contest with predetermined winners.

Audiences consisted of the friends and family of said popularity winners and their church friends. It's cute and fun certainly. I was involved briefly but quickly grew tired of the high school feel of it all and resigned from their board of directors shortly after being asked to join. They undoubtedly serve a good purpose for the community. I just found that the proverbial chairs at the table were limited.

When we first moved to Zanesville nearly ten years ago, this town felt like a sanctuary. It was the place we escaped to when I lost my parents. It was my "anywhere else but here" place. I have spent many hours journaling, crying, talking, and processing.

Now I am finally understanding. Zanesville has been so important for me to find a quiet place to heal but, with few exceptions, not to find meaningful connections. Zanesville has only been painful when I tried to make it something it wasn't. It's been a great place to rest. It really has. I just can't stay here long-term.

As many people do, I deal with the ghosts of personal trauma, and they affect how I move around in the world and, more importantly, how I am able to connect to people.

I have noticed many changes in my perception as I find myself in my late 50's. It's still a mystery to me, for example, how my inner 24-year-old self stands in front of the mirror observing the 56-year-old version of myself. The wrinkles around my eyes, the increasing number of grey hairs, the few extra pounds, and colonoscopy appointments all remind me of where I am. These things used to embarrass me until I realized there are people whom I have loved dearly who no longer have the privilege to be alive.

When I look at it through that lens, the extra pounds mean I've established a meaningful career and have been able to feed myself. The wrinkles remind me of the precious summer hours I've spent outside with my kids. The health screenings serve to help keep me cancer-free for as long as possible. My fragile, youthful vanity is now fading as I embrace a new comfort in my new reality. I've shifted priorities. I've changed, certainly, but I believe we're supposed to. We are supposed to grow and evolve. When we stop growing and learning, we die.

One of the many things I am no longer comfortable with is the word mistake. To me, it implies we did something wrong. It also implies that the opposite of wrong is right or, even more problematic, perfect. The concept creates a standard, an expectation. More and more communities are starting to ask the question: Why can't I just be?

Life gets messy, on purpose, I think. How else would we learn? Seriously, think about it. As children, if we fell asleep with gum in our mouths, we learned quickly the humility of that unfortunate haircut the next day.

Now that we're all grown up, we learn about relationships, how to navigate conflict with people. It's all a learning process. There is no real end to that.

Very few things in this world are simplistic; therefore, I don't think life always fits into the paradigm of right and wrong. The world is full of grey areas. I think pretending we live in a world that is so binary and simple is naïve and ultimately causes harm. We all trip and stumble through life in our own awkward way.

Most of us have life choices we look back on with regret and shame. Sometimes that regret is the kind that seeps into our pores and convinces us that we are pieces of shit.

My self-discovery has not always been pretty. Sometimes, I have learned things about myself that made me feel shame. Self-forgiveness has been somewhat like grabbing a cloud, but I am working on it.

I present this to you not as a totally healed person. I'm not. I present it from a version of myself that's hopefully a bit wiser and more insightful.

I'm still healing.

My goal is to be a better person than I was the day before. Often, I fall short. Often, I fall on my face. That's ok. I get up and I try again. My desire to help lessen suffering through education and compassion.

So this is where I've landed.

As a queer kid I learned early how to edit myself for the comfort of others and when I could make the adults in my life, happy, then my life got easier. As I got older, I was often complimented for my maturity at my age. I wasn't more mature than my peers. I just became an expert at masking my needs.

But enough about me now. Now, let me tell you how I got here.

Chapter Two
Edna

The people in my family have a very indirect way of communicating.

The details of my birth and early childhood and the origins of my family are things I have pieced together over the years anecdotally. Few people in my family ever sat down and explained or communicated directly about most of this. Getting all the facts about anything in my family was like trying to catch all the brine shrimp in the aquarium with only one scoop of the net. You'll never get them all, and the more you scoop, the more they scatter.

The following is a mosaic of what I have pieced together. Some pieces are a matter of fact, as I understand; some are a matter of reasonable assumption, and some are perception. In any case, it's all valid because I was the one who experienced them.

Here's what I think I know.

My Mom had just turned 16 the month before I was born. My Dad had just turned 18 only a week before that. I was frail and underweight because I was born two months early. My father got a draft waiver from the Vietnam war because I was not expected to live through the night. Doctors suggested that my parents contact a local funeral home to prepare for my death. My father described it as my lungs being like two layers of wet Kleenex. The only way I was going to survive was to get air into them without tearing them, and that possibility was not hopeful.

I stayed in the hospital for two months. Even my newborn picture featured a two-month-old me. I looked like a tiny little wrinkled old man. There are no photos of me as a newborn.

I have often wondered why I survived. I mean, I'm glad I did, but there was no medical reason. I just as easily could have died. Is this the resilience of the human spirit? Is there some cosmic purpose? I don't know. I just figure, after all this time, if I have survived everything that I have, the least I can do is talk about it and explain what I've learned. So much of my understanding comes after spending years in family systems and patterns of behavior that I didn't even understand, much less had any awareness I was participating in.

As a kid and as a teen, I felt like my world was constantly shaken up like a snow globe. There was calm, and there were times of beauty, but that calm was always short-lived and was inevitably disturbed by someone or something.

A retrospective view has helped me understand my family's behavior and my reaction to it. I mean, hurt people hurt people, right? My parents had their own experience with their childhoods and certainly adopted toxic traits, parenting techniques, etc., and it all trickles down. What we don't correct or process simply flows down to the next generation like hot lava. I maintain that my feelings are valid, but I no longer need to stay in my head about it. I can crawl out.

My parents both came from poor Appalachian families who saw little value in education. I think that's one of the reasons I found Zanesville to be so nostalgic for the good parts of my childhood. My father's family is from Tennessee. Dysfunctional family values were as thick as meatloaf gravy.

My paternal grandmother's maiden name was Hatfield, from the original Hatfield family of the legendary Hatfields and McCoys. For readers who are not familiar with the name, here a bit of back story:

The infamous feud between the Hatfield and McCoy families, which lasted from the late 1800s into the early 1900s, is one of the most famous family conflicts in American history. The exact cause of the feud is a mix of fact and folklore. But there are several key events believed to have sparked and fueled the hostility, including but not limited to: civil war allegiances, land disputes, and romantic entanglements. But perhaps the most telling of folklore conflicts within this family was the hog incident.

It's one of the most well-documented early flashpoints occurred in 1878, when Randolph McCoy accused Floyd Hatfield of stealing one of his hogs. At the time, hogs were a valuable commodity, and the dispute went to court. A jury composed of members from both families ruled in favor of the Hatfields, further straining relations.

Many historians agree that the cause for the feud between the two families was not clear. Even the cause of that conflict itself was something that many of them fought and died over.

As I grew up, I often pondered the parallels in how my family dealt with conflict and the Apalachin folklore of these two families. From a sociological standpoint, I see similar patterns in communication styles.

Conflict seldom involved civility. Standing out as an individual while maintaining an unwavering loyalty to one's biological family was frowned upon, and direct clear communication was substituted for tenacious family gossip. I sometimes felt like my family operated much like a swarming wasp nest, which is fine, as long as you're a wasp.

My grandmother's name was Edna. She had a third-grade education and had a fairly limited social development as a result. Her father made her quit school to help more at home with her siblings. In her culture family was valued above all else, above education, above convenience and certainly above self. Anyone who was not family were defined as outsiders.

Later I would learn that this is actually a very common Appalachian trait. The problem I see with this blind loyalty is that while it can create a safe haven and support system, it can also create life sentence of exposure to toxic behavior because that's what families do and if that's all you know, that's all you know.

Edna was a cunning, manipulative old woman. She surrounded herself with whirlwinds of gossip. Then, taking the stage as the victim of said gossip. In our large family, the game of telephone was a very easy one to get started. You could end up with all kinds of creative tales about yourself by the end of the day. The truth or factual content was secondary at best. The version of the story she would tell was a warped and twisted rendition of something not even resembling the truth. She literally kept an old address book by her rotary phone and bottles of pink nail polish. Next to her collection of nail polish bottles sat a plastic cup which held about 100 ball point pens, of which only a few worked. Her black plastic address book held all of the contacts of everyone in the family. Her gossip was, at best, peppered with lies and sometimes outright outlandish slander of her own creation. She was the source of many family fights.

One glaring example went something like this:

My parents were just married. My mom was 17 at the time. Edna was most certainly not a fan of my mother because she felt Mom had stolen her 'baby' away from her.

One day, while my father was at work, Edna called Mom on the phone. She told my mom she was nothing but a whore! I'm sure other colorful language was exchanged! Now, my father was somewhat of a mama's boy so any woman in my mothers position would have gotten the same treatment. Mom was not the kind of person to not fight back so she called my dad at work to tell him what had just happened. Before mom was able to get dad on the phone, Edna had already reached dad and told him that my mother was the one who had called her and cussed her out! It must have been quite the performance because my dad never backed my mom and they fought about that phone call for many years after that.

Edna intentionally went out of her way to create conflict among many of us. She also was the same person who would whine and complain that no one would come visit her. Her levels of vindictiveness knew no limits and any semblance of truth often was not present in any way. It was entertainment.

Over the years only the most dysfunctional people in my family were drawn to Edna. The rest of us tolerated the awkward family events.

There was always a cousin or two who lived in one of the back bedrooms who needed a place to stay till they got on their feet. So, they often added to the drama under that safe roof.

We used to joke that a person could show up at Edna's door with a needle in their arm and she would offer them a place to stay. Most of my life I thought this was simply an example of a kind and compassionate heart. Her behaviors often had a shimmer of charity but she invariably had an agenda. I suppose I'll never know her true intentions. I'll tell you what I do know though: She used those same peoples stories as fodder for her gossip, proof of her alleged goodness and an endless supply of dysfunction to engage in. It was all she knew. When she got bored, she'd create more.

This veil of charitable energy was no more apparent than the countless years she spent being a foster parent. There were more children in and out of that home than anyone could possibly count. A relative, friend or case worker of any one of them were often coming or going through that screen door at any given hour.

The transient energy in that house was so dense. Even as her own grandson, upon entering her house, I was often met with wide eyed stares from any one of the disheveled teens, as if they were saying, "Who the fuck are you?" After a few years of her fostering, the energy took over that house and it was no longer my quirky grandmothers home but a hub to where they all were going, coming or lingering.

Were there worse foster homes? Absolutely. Was Edna a good foster parent? Absolutely not. While it was true that many of theses children had come from violent situations with horrific circumstances, Edna's house was not much better sometimes.

The chaos and void of coping skills the foster children brought with them, fit neatly in Edna's house and she fed off of it as much as it overwhelmed her. She would take any child, any age, who came from any circumstances.

As a licensed social worker, I often wonder what the hell these case workers were thinking when placing certain children with her.

I remember she once took in a 16-year-old girl whose parents, brother and sister had all been murdered by her boyfriend. The young girl didn't help pull the trigger but she did help her boyfriend plan it and told him exactly when they would all be home so he could kill them. The plan was to kill her family so she could run away with her boyfriend. They were both captured at a greyhound bus station. This girl was so terribly troubled and traumatized she suffered from hallucinations where she'd see her dead parents in her room at night. Years after the girl left my grandmothers house, Edna remained pen pals with the boyfriend on death row and accepted all collect phone calls from prison.

There was a certain kind of kid who could do well in her home and certain children who would not. I remember once she had an African American teen removed by the police who had *mysteriously* become violent. What she failed to mention to the officer was that she had told the child: "If you don't want be called a fucking n**ger, then stop acting

14

like one!"

This was her source of income clearly and she made no qualms about admitting that. I remember once she told me, right in front of a little boy who sat quietly on the couch: "Thanks to that one sittin' over there", as she pointed in his direction, "I can get me them new kitchen cabinets!'

Her simplicity makes her sound like a monster, I know. The truth is, although she could be outright mean when she wanted to be, in instances such as this, she really was that simple and had no idea what she was saying was rude or insensitive in any way.

Keep in mind, she had a 3rd grade education. If you consider the lack of emotional regulation a 3rd grader typically has, that was Edna. She said exactly what was on her mind and made no apologies for it. Sometimes there was even a wave of completely inappropriate humor you got by listening to her. Not that it was funny per se, but it was much like watching a sit-com character so grossly over the top, having no idea they were actually the butt of the joke. She was a caricature.

I remember once watching her pick up the receiver to her rotary phone with a loving smile on her face: "Oh hi honey! How are you? I was just prayin for you! Honey, I ..." then, turning her mouth only inches from the mouth piece, she screamed: "Katrina, get off that goddamn trampoline or Ill break your goddamn neck!!" Then, barely missing a beat, the smile would creep back on her face and she continued, "Oh honey these damned kids are driving me crazy!" then she'd chuckle.

The reference I often use to describe Edna was like the character "Mama" played by Vicki Lawrence from "Mamas family". Just add some colorful racism, less wisdom and a few F bombs and you'd have Edna Marlow.

After these explosive episodes of emotional dysregulation, she'd grab her prescription bottle filled with her nerve pills as she called them. I would learn later her nerve pills were more commonly known as benzodiazepines, for which she had an endless supply..

She had the patience of a child, the impulse control of a teenager and the mouth of a drunk. Yet, once in a while without warning, she'd offer some sincere emotional support, like her reaction when I came out to her.

"Now you listen to me!", she said, shaking her finger at me. "I'll tell you what! Your daddy is just gonna have to git over his shit! It ain't like you're the only one in the world who's like that! Now, if ya were, we'd string ya up, but cha ain't!"

Then she smiled as she patted my knee.

You might think I hated her. I didn't. I loved her. I didn't always like her, but I loved her. She intrigued me. I just learned that I had to love her from a distance.

She also had a wicked and often macabre sense of humor that just made it hard not to giggle. She was a true bitch and had loyalty to very few. Anyone could be her next target.

It was how she thrived. It was who she was. I sometimes loved the idea of her because she was my grandmother.

I loved listening to her stories about her childhood. She was a phenominal story teller! She gave all her characters voice and her vocabulary and experssions were an example of part of Apalachin culture that I will always love. Its simple. Its rich.

She shared chilling stories about seeing ghosts in the hills of Tennessee. Most of her tales were weaved with a mystical Appalachian folklore so eerie and compelling. I'd sit wide eyed on that plastic covered couch draped with one of her granny square afgans. In the early years, it was actually covered in plastic, as was the culture in the late 70's. This matched the hard plastic walkway that covered high traffic areas on the carpet.

I remember visualing the shadowy supernatural images in her stories. I imaged ghostly images barely visable in the fog of the Smokey Mountains where she grew up. I remember tales of deceased loved ones who'd allegedly come to people in dreams to predict life events or to provide comfort after a sudden death. It was mystifying, comforting and scary as shit all at the same time. Maybe she was talking about ghosts only seen in the peripheral of one's eye, power of suggestion perhaps. Her stories were a reminder that the mountains and hallows of those Tennessee hills held unexplained mysteries and dark secrets. I found the narratives about her adventures intoxicating. I wanted them all to be true.

Edna was a toxic person who I honestly do not miss. I recall countelss times wanting to feel closer to that witchy version of her. I wanted desperately to find the wisdom in her superstition and hold tightly to the traditions of her culture that felt so magical. Trying to isolate those mysterious parts of her life from the truly abusive pernicious parts was like trying to seperate all the colors of playdough once you've mixed them together. It simply wasn't possible

Sadly the veil of mystic culture became increasingly thin as I got older to reveal an old redneck woman who's two most compelling features were her heavenly creamy peanutbutter fudge, and the golf ball sized bunions on the inside of both her feet.

It made me sad to realize she was just a mean old vendictive woman who loved scaring children, and who found enjoyment in causing conflict and turmoil in the very people she claimed to love.

The truth is that Edna had the potential to be unwaveringly cruel and achieved a certain satisfaction in her self-educed dramas. In all my years as a psychotherapist I've never met another person like her. Even my father, who was a toxic son of a bitch, was a poor reproduction. Edna Marlow was a classic.

Chapter Three
The Roots

My family, as a whole, is a stereotypical hot mess of Southern tradition, Southern Baptist roots, and a shroud of conservative values that no more matched their behavior than an onion pretending to be an apple.

Now, when Edna was a small child, her mother, Amanda Hatfield, had started a big scandal in their little town of Jellico, Tennessee.

Similar to most women of that time, Great Grandma Amanda was a simple, humble woman. Her culture dictated submissiveness and soft-spokenness as virtues. She was not known to wear makeup or dress nicely. This was most likely due to the fact that they were so poor.

As the story goes, Amanda's behavior began to change one summer.

She began wearing lipstick, make-up, and making fancy dresses she would wear when she went into town, which she did alone.

Shortly thereafter, she began a romantic relationship with another woman and left my great-grandfather, Jake Hatfied.

. It was a story I was not told until I was an adult, but through some research, I found to be 100% true. The story goes that Amanda ran off with her lesbian lover and left poor old Jake with a house full of kids. Edna says that he offered to build a house for the two women a house just up the hill so they could all raise the kids together. This is the only part of the story I have not been able to verify but I find this version of hillbilly polyamory so intriguing.

This story was my first data point that sexual orientation in my opinion, has a genetic origin.

Jake remarried a woman named Bessie. She was a kind, gentle woman with a quite soft spoken demeanor. I knew great grandma Bessie only briefly. She died when I was in grade school but I have fond memories of sitting on her lap hearing her soft whispery voice. She so was frail and skinny. Her hands were like boney fingers wrapped in a thin layer of skin that seemed no more than wrinkly tissue paper. I remember looking up at her while she spoke because her voice was so faint, even as I was sitting in her lap.

It was then I'd notice her mouth full of putrid brown juice known as snuff. She kept an open folgers coffee tin on the floor next to her rocking chair that she would occasionally lean over my head to spit into.

My father was the oldest of 7 children. He was also a twin. Edna had no idea she was pregnant with twins. Back in those days births happened at home. She saved up for a whole month until she had the $20 for the doctor to come out for the delivery. She was relieved when the doctor didn't charge her extra for the second baby, which later, she confessed she was worried about.

Knowing what I know about that woman now, I can't imagine her parenting an infant, let alone seven of them, but she did. Well, by today's standards, I'm not so sure I'd use the word parenting. She did keep them alive, though.

In retrospect, I see now that each of Edna's seven children developed their own version of simple-minded southern dysfunction. Some of my uncles were much better at it than others, adding new ingredients like addiction, incarceration and abuse to their repertoire.

I'll will never know the degree of multigenerational trauma my grandmother was undoubtably a part of. She watched her brother get killed by a train right in front of her, for example. Oddly, trains were a major cause of death in my family. Her father, Jake, was hit and killed by a train.

A cousin passed out drunk in a train tunnel while walking home from a bar, was also killed by a train.

In my macabe humor it makes me picture these drunken Appalachian folks stumbling around too drunk to stay off the damn train tracks! I'll go to hell for that one, but I stand by it.

My mothers family was from Kentucky. Like my father's family, mom's family also held a deep connection to their Appalachian heritage. They were just as poverty stricken but there was something about my moms family that put them just a touch above my dads in terms of class. They were a little more connected to the real world and a tad bit less dysfunctional in some ways. As I pause in my thoughts while writing this, I think the main difference was I felt genuine love and acceptance from my mother's family. I felt seen in a way I never did with Ednas family. I say that with no judgement. It just makes sense.

Like many families in the south and midwest, my mother's family prided themselves in their antidotal belief that we were partially of Native American descent. Any readers not from the Midwest may not realize what a cliché this is but it is something you hear in more Appalachian families than not.

DNA results in recent years revealed that our darker skin and black hair had no connection to Native American heritage whatsoever but rather to Cuban descent. Although we were raised in a midwest white bread culture, Latino heritage would be a part of my history that I would resonate with, creating a strong yearning and unexplained connection

Mom was the second oldest of 7 children. I think mom felt lost in her family. She wasn't seen. The only way she knew to get attention was to act out. I know she ran away more than once and I believe was in juvenile detention at some point. Again, no judgement. Its all she knew.

Meeting my father was also an escape from her own abusive mother.

She had dropped out of school at 15 as a sophomore to give birth to me. She later earned her GED when I was in kindergarten. I remember telling my teacher one day that I was going to my moms high school graduation. She was sure I was confused and meant to say sister instead of my mother.

Mom started her adult life at 15 years old. Limited education and generational poverty were part of her foundation. With very few exceptions I can honestly say she really did do the best she could with what she had. I resonated deeply with my moms family. Their dysfunction was different that dads side of the family. It was just as obvious as dad's family, but somehow I felt like I was an organic part of it with moms family. I closely resemble my mom and her parents. Seeing young pictures of my grandfather was like looking in the mirror. Mom and I passed for siblings on several occasions in my teenage years. I was one of them. The connection needed no explanation.

My grandfather loved the outdoors. In his own vocabulary, he taught me about the importance of ecosystems, wildlife and medicinal uses for trees and plants. The false narrative of native American heritage was easy to believe. The things he taught me are very much the foundation of some of the nature work I do today, as a psychotherapist.

I remember a warm summer day in Kentucky. I ran across the porch where he was sitting. I stopped abruptly and proudly stomped my foot as hard as I could, deliberately killing a large wolf spider. I wanted his praise for being brave enough to kill it but it bothered him that I enjoyed killing it. He didn't shame me, but he was stern. I sheepishly apologized as he explained the spider did nothing to me and I had no right to kill it. He told me how spiders eat mosquitos and flies and how, in that way, they are good to have around. In his own simple way, he explained symbiosis in real time.

He taught me that people are not separate from nature. We are a part of it. I learned from him how to find the rhythm between people and their natural world.

We spent most of our summers in Kentucky at my grandparents property near Lake Cumberland. The nights I spent outside with him around that campfire were the most precious. During the day, my grandmother would throw all food scraps over the hill from their trailer into the woods. At night, with my grandfather, Id stay up late and listen for the rustling of leaves as raccoons, opossums and foxes helped themselves to the scraps. Sitting there in the darkness I remember feeling mesmerized as we tried to match the sounds we were hearing to the unseen animals scavenging around just out of sight. The occasional flash of shiny eyes in the dark or a growl made us wonder if we were being visited by a fox or maybe a coyote. It was magical.

Applying what I now know as an adult, I understand how people experience healing and peace in natural settings. My grandfather has been dead for many years. I sometimes wonder if somewhere in some parallel universe, he and I aren't still sitting out by that fire.

Chapter Four
Florida

Typically, any time we got to go somewhere exciting it was to Kentucky or Tennessee to visit mom or dads family. That was the perimeter of our vacations. One summer, when I was in grade school mom and dad were able to plan a trip to Disney World. Florida may as well have been the carribean, for all I knew. It was the most exotic place I'd ever been! I'm still not sure how they did it. I know we never had a surplus of money because of how we lived, so this was something I never forgot.

Dad had one of those lightweight aluminum cabs tightly secured to his pickup truck. My sister and I rode all the way to Florida on route 70 lying in the back. This was long before seatbelts were required. I don't remember exactly but I can only assume it must have been lined with sleeping bags and blankets. I remember it was cozy. Dad had built wooden shelves that lined each side of the inside of that cab. Mom stocked it with canned food, condiments and loaves of bread. I don't see it in my mind, but Im certain that somewhere there was also likely a cooler with lunch meat and bologna. No need to stop for fast food. We had all we needed.

One of the most magical parts of the trip was the new walkie talkies dad got from Radio Shack. I was amazed that we could press that little button on the right side and talk right through the glass window! Not only was this years before the first Atari video game, but even before pong, so it was truly a big deal.

I have no memory of the actual drive but I do remember how Florida felt like pure paradise once we got there. We stayed in an actual motel with a small pool and a little outdoor shower. It was my first time staying anywhere that wasn't my house or a relatives house. I still have a picture of my sister and I standing in front of a little lime tree growing in the side yard. I was certain we had won the lottery or something. I have a vague memory of some kind of electric parade or something with mickey mouse and friends which totally freaked me out, but that little lime tree next to the pool? Now, that's what's I called a vacation!

The motel must have been in some kind of proximity to the beach because I also have a memory of being at the ocean, and much to the frustration of my parents, I was scared to death! My fear, almost hysteria really, was a mystery at first, until mom figured out that just before our trip to Florida that my parents had worked so hard to make happen, Edna, in her parental wisdom, had let us all watch the original JAWS. I was convinced our little trip to paradise would end with us all being eaten by a giant shark, leaving nothing but bloody water and mangled body parts.

Chapter Five
Timothy

My mother's second baby, like me, was also born two months early and had similar issues with his lungs and his heart. He was allegedly stronger than I was, but his little heart would flutter and skip and just couldn't keep a rhythm, so he died.

My mother said she would sit by his incubator and hold him. While she rubbed the small of his back, his heart would beat normally, but as soon as she would lie him down, his heartbeat would flutter. She says, still to this day, that she wished she never would have laid him back down.

The pain in her voice never went away over the years on the rare occasions she tells this story.

Timothy's funeral was my first memory. If I close my eyes, I can still smell the flowers. The only photo I have come across over the years is one of me standing behind the hearse, holding this spray of flowers that was bigger than I was.

It's still odd to me to reflect on what I actually remember because my understanding was limited. In fact, I remember being kind of excited because my entire family was together in one place! That almost never happened! Not only were all my aunts, uncle and cousins there but a host of extended family from Kentucky and Tennessee as well.

I recall thinking it was odd that everyone seemed so sad. I didn't understand what dead meant. I only knew mom was pregnant, then she wasn't, then she came home from the hospital. End of story.

I also remember feeling a bit ignored. I could see many adults hugging and whispering in hushed voices.

I remember Dad trying not to cry.

I was only two, but I remember it distinctly. I remember seeing my dad's bottom lip quiver and eventually the tears fell.

Part of my father's grief was attached to the fact that Timothy had strong physical features from his side of the family. Timothy was a fair-skinned baby with blonde hair. He was everything I wasn't.

I, on the other hand, strongly resemble my mother's family. My dad never forgave me for not inheriting his family's physical traits.

I remember holding my dad's oversized, callused hands as we walked through the clusters of people chattering and whispering. I couldn't even see where we were going because of my limited view. A few more steps and the crowd thinned as we reached the front of the room. I saw that little white box surrounded by fragrant flowers and tacky ribbons. I could barely see over the edge of my brother's casket, but I remember placing my hands on the top edge of the side of it so I could pull myself up a bit to see his face while I stood on my toes. I can still see his little face. He was so still.. So very still. I remember saying:

"Daddy, Baby dead?"

Dad's tears turned to sobs. I never saw him cry like that ever again. Something in my dad broke that day, and I don't think he was ever able to fix it.

I remember wanting someone to talk to me, play with me, or something. My mom was like a zombie for months after that.

I've asked her, as an adult, how she survived that or why she never got any counseling. She said, "My baby died. We buried him and came home. That's just what people did in those days."

It was the 70s. It wasn't the stone ages. I think there was just so much stigma against mental health, even more than today, that it never occurred to her to get help.

The day he died, she stayed in the hospital overnight in the maternity ward, hearing the other babies cry. She eventually requested to be temporarily moved up to the psych ward. A part of her heart hardened that day, and it never softened. As long as I live, no matter what they have done to me, I'll always hold a place in my heart for that version of my mother.

Approximately 7 years later, mom wanted to do some responsible end-of-life planning for the future and purchase her own plot. Not surprisingly, her primary concern was that she be buried next to her child, a reasonable request for any grieving mother. That kind of loss becomes a part of your identity.

Unbeknownst to my parents, they had buried Timothy in a part of the cemetery designated exclusively for children. This was unacceptable. I have no idea what kinds of legal difficulty they faced to accomplish it, but they had my brother exhumed and moved to a different cemetery where they purchased plots of their own on either side of my brother. This happened a number of years after his death.

While I cannot say I wouldn't make the same decision in my mother's place, it had to be a difficult decision to make. The details of this event are only what I pieced together in my mind. No one ever explained it to me until I was older, and only then because I asked the right questions.

Even though I was very young, my mind was often fixated on Timothy and what it meant to have a dead brother. Anytime I was scolded or caused my parents pain, I remembered the stories of my own predicted death and Timothy's predicted survival. It left me with some very heavy thoughts.

The day of the exhumation, I was dressed in my little plaid suit. My parents, my sister, and I gathered at the grave. We were all dressed nicely, just like the memories I had of the original funeral. In contrast to that day, however, there were no fresh carnations or crowds of people, just us. No music or words of comfort. We stood at the grave that had been dug open. A perfectly shaped mound of fresh, warm brown dirt was piled next to the hole where my brother had been. That same tiny white box sat on top of the ground nearby. I still have the photograph my mother took that day, my sister and I kneeling beside an empty hole in the ground. A poignant moment was etched in my mind. That was the moment I was reminded it should have been me in that box. It should have been me.

The new cemetery had a policy that only allowed headstones that were flush to the ground. The headstone we had for him was a raised one that we could not reuse.

My parents purchased a new flat placard for my brother, which featured a bronze image of Jesus sitting with a small child on his lap.

The old headstone no longer served a purpose, but my parents didn't know what to do with it. Subsequently, that stone bearing my brother's name sat in our garage next to the gasoline can. The stone remained there for my entire childhood. Anytime I entered the garage to get my bicycle or a rake, I was met with the cold reminder: I shouldn't be here. Although we never talked about it, that message rang in my ears my entire life.

I think there is a lot of normality in kids comparing themselves to other kids. In my case, I was comparing myself to a dead kid who could make no mistakes. He was perfect.

I believe that my parents reminded me of these events in an effort to instill a sense of gratitude. I don't know, but it haunted me.

Later in life on several occasions, my father would be hyper critical of me for my opinions, my beliefs, and even my identity. So often I wondered if maybe the wrong child had died.

My sister was my best friend. I was rarely annoyed by her existence as many older brothers were by their younger sisters. Perhaps it was because of the loss of my brother, I don't know, but I was always extremely protective of her.

She too was fair-skinned baby with blonde hair.

My family made me feel like I was the luckiest little boy to be alive and I grew up hearing the stories of my miraculous survival. These stories sometimes made me feel like I was something special, or more acutely that someday I would be someone special. As I grew, those emotions of guilt for taking up space would have a strong influence on the adult I would become. Birthdays and Christmases often brought a sense of survivor's guilt. My father's judgement about what kind of son I should be reinforced that feeling.

When the Bedbugs Bite

Chapter Six
The Fox

My parents' first house was a rented two-story home in Englewood, Ohio, on a few acres of land. We lived there from the time I was an infant until I was 12. I loved that house. So much of my life there contributed to my core values. It was a densely wooded property with a small creek that ran through it. Most days, I could be found outside, usually in the woods, looking for crawdads, worms, frogs, or snakes. My mom used to say that she hated checking my pockets before doing laundry because she would sometimes find those same worms, frogs, and snakes.

Wandering through the woods felt like I was visiting friends. It was where I felt safe. It was also where I found what I now consider to be my spirit animal.

I was kneeling by the creek, watching the minnows dart in and out of their cloudy hiding places. I heard a tiny sound, the crunching sound of a dead leaf. My head shot up. The rest of my body remained kneeling at the creek's edge, my hands still in the water. There, in front of me, no more than 20 feet away, stood a beautiful red fox who had come to the creek for a drink. He was staring at me. He was cautious, motionless. He looked directly at me. His eyes were vibrant and intense. They met mine with a calculating intention. I did the same. I remember thinking "Holy shit! It's a real fox!" I sometimes wonder if he was thinking "Holy shit! It's a boy!" Breathless and frozen, I looked back into his face. I didn't want to do anything to frighten him. He looked fake, as if someone had placed him there to look real. That fox and I stared at one another for only about 10 seconds, but I remember every moment of that experience like it was yesterday.

Without warning, the fox very slowly turned around and walked silently back into the woods from where he had come. He wasn't scared or aggressive. He simply shared that space with me there in the woods for a moment and now only in my mind.

I didn't have a lot of friends as a child. I was okay with it. It never felt like a deficiency. Both my mom and dad had come from families of seven children, so I had a massive network of peers through the many cousins from all of my aunts and uncles. Having friends outside of that social network was not only not encouraged, it was just unnecessary and felt foreign. It simply never occurred to me.

I had no idea how poor we were. When I think back about that house, I remember the living room had a short-ply grey carpet with large, oddly shaped black areas where the carpet had been worn down past the threads and through to the floorboards. I remember the first time I noticed the fact that some of my cousins did not have these patterns in their carpets like ours. It was one of the first times I became consciously aware of our socioeconomic status. I remember thinking that people who didn't have these patterns in their carpet must think they were better than us. I would later more accurately identify that experience as embarrassment.

My father had factory jobs. He also had that same pickup truck and kept an ad running in the classified section of the local newspaper where he provided hauling services: trash, furniture, anything. I remember many of my Saturday morning cartoons were ruined by having to accompany my father to the city dump to unload trash he had hauled for someone. I don't have a lot of memories of Saturday morning cartoons. In those days, there was no cable or satellite TV, just a handful of local channels, assuming, of course, your TV antenna worked. There was no recording shows. You watched what was airing when it was on or you didn't see it.

When I wasn't accompanying my father to trips to the dump, I have memories of Saturday morning cartoons being cancelled for an extended period of time due to something called Watergate. I had no idea what it was. I was just annoyed that I felt cheated out of my cartoons more often than not.

Like many families, my parents had very distinct ideas about gender norms and gender identity. There were certainly boys' toys and girls' toys. Even today, in any store, there are distinct isles of blue including toy trucks and tools and isles of pink including kitchen sets and tiny vacuum cleaners. One day in between my Bugs Bunny cartoons, I saw a commercial for something I felt would make my life complete: An easy-bake oven! I was fascinated! I had to have one. I made sure it was at the top of my list for Santa that year! I remember distinctly my father's face when I revealed what was on my list for the jolly old man. Dad looked at Mom and rolled his eyes. Clearly, he was not happy with my choice.

I had helped my mom make brownies and cookies many times. I had been allowed to lick the beaters from the mixer, lick the spoon, crack the eggs, all of it. But something about my having the little oven to do the baking just sounded magical to me! Christmas morning smelled like pine needles and coffee, the way it always did. I should've been happy. I wanted to be happy. But when I tore the paper off the long, heavy box, my stomach sank so hard it felt like it might fall right through the floor. It wasn't the Easy-Bake Oven I'd been dreaming about for weeks. It was a shotgun. A real, cold, heavy shotgun. I froze, staring at it, trying to figure out how to make my face look excited.

"Now you're a real man," Dad said, smiling like he'd just handed me the greatest gift in the world. His hand clapped hard against my back, and I flinched.

I looked down at the gun again, my hands trembling as I picked it up. It felt wrong in every way. I wanted to throw it across the room, but instead, I nodded and forced the words out of my mouth. "Thanks, Dad." My voice cracked, but he didn't seem to notice. I kept the fake smile plastered on my face all morning, but inside, I was breaking.

I'd wanted that little oven so badly—not because it was for girls or anything, but because it was perfect. It was mine. I'd imagined baking tiny cakes and decorating them with swirls of frosting, like I'd seen on the commercials. It made me happy just thinking about it. But now, standing there holding a weapon I didn't want, I realized Dad would never see me the way I was. He didn't want me to be me.

Later, I locked myself in the bathroom and sat on the edge of the toilet, clutching a towel to my face to muffle the sounds of me crying. I cried for the oven I'd never get, but mostly, I cried because even on Christmas morning, my dad's love felt like a reminder of everything I wasn't.

After my brother died, my father became a self-proclaimed religious man. In hindsight, I think my mother went along with it because going to church was something you were just supposed to do. Much like the work ethic, being a Christian, and in particular one who attends church regularly, provided an instant morality rating. I think the fact that they were both grieving the death of a child also made it the only place they knew to turn for comfort. The reality of having a dead child, I think, can only be dampened by the notion that somewhere that child is safe and happy living with an all-loving god up in the clouds. An all-loving and all-knowing God, who, in his great wisdom, killed an innocent child, destroying the heart and soul of his parents forever. I will never understand that.

I have spent a lifetime wondering what kind of people my parents would have become had my brother lived. Having to bury a child most certainly changes a person. It leaves a scar on your soul that defines an awful, unspeakable moment in time.

Aside from stories told to me about my birth and how lucky I was, we rarely spoke of my brother. I don't ever recall my father going to his grave. Perhaps he did, but I have no memory of it. My mother visited the grave three times a year. She would place a wreath on Timothy's grave every Christmas, Memorial Day, and his birthday. This happened my entire life without fail. To the best of my knowledge, it still does.

Chapter Seven
Divorce

My parents divorced when I was 12, and they both remarried. My father had become a complete right-wing religious nut. He was morally gross. He and his wife had a moral priority to make sure everyone in the community knew of their status as Christians, perhaps to compensate for how they actually conducted their lives. I don't pretend to know.

My father was there every time the church doors opened. He volunteered for every event, sang in the church choir, wrote and directed all Christmas plays, and even drove the church bus to recruit children whose parents couldn't drive them to church. It was his purpose.

He was also an ignorant racist who had no empathy or compassion for anyone who didn't look or believe as he did. My dad was a smart, creative man in many regards. His ignorance was the worst because it was willful.

My mother was not at all religious but had married a man who was extraordinarily abusive to her and to us. I recall a random moment in 5th grade when he informed me:

"If you ever come home with a ni**er or a queer, you'll no longer be welcome here."

He was a blob of a man, not just in stature but in the weight of his unchecked rage. His towering frame housed a spirit as petulant as a spoiled child. His temper, swollen with ignorance, would erupt over the most minor confusion, a tempest of red-faced rage and flailing fists. The walls of our home had memorized the symphony of his tantrums— the crash of shattered dishes, the dull thud of bruised skin meeting unyielding force. In his world, understanding was an inconvenience, a thing to be met with fists rather than thought. But fear—fear was something we all understood.

He'd taunt me and verbally tease me for being too skinny or weak. He loved to see fear in my face and would even snicker when I trembled.

He compensated for how insecure he felt intellectually with a seething temper. He referred to Martin Luther King day as either "Coon day" or "James Earl Ray day." Each year, he would sneer at the fact that we got a day off from school that day. I can still recall him making fun of the "I have a dream" speech on TV as he formed his hand and index finger into the shape of a gun and pretended to shoot the image of MLK on the screen. We often had fist-sized holes in our walls accompanied by the sounds of breaking glass and the screaming cliches of, "LOOK WHAT YOU MADE ME DO!!"

We were all terrified of him, all the time, and he loved it. It made him feel powerful. There are few people on this planet who I hope experience slow agonizing deaths but he is one of them.

He had a tissue-paper ego so fragile that the slightest thing could trigger him. It could be someone's opinion, someone's words, or sometimes even the fact that certain people were allowed to exist.

I used to think there were moments when he exhibited an ounce of emotional maturity or respect. For example, when my mother would visit my brother's grave, he and my mother would drive out to the cemetery, he would stay in the car while she spent a little time at her son's grave. He said he remained in the car out of respect because it wasn't his child, so he gave mom that privacy to pay her respect on her own. This made sense on the surface.

The reality, however, is that he was forcibly enmeshed in every moment and every aspect of my mom's life. It's much more likely that since her grief had nothing to do with him, he saw no reason to give her any support. It wasn't his child and wasn't his problem. It wasn't respect. It was indifference. He could not have cared less. She didn't drive the 15 minutes to the cemetery on her own. No, he had to go with her, so he could sit in the car.

This was a man who constantly and relentlessly would text her if she left the house without him. If she went to the grocery store, he would text or call asking how fast she was driving, where she should stop for gas, which route he thought she should take to get there and once she arrived, he'd text again, asking which aisle of the store she was in and what time she would be back. Not a single moment passed in her life that was not authorized by him. No, this was not a man who gave her any space to exist. Her dead child had nothing to do with him; therefore, in his eyes, it was not important.

He may have had a massive stature, but that stature was compensation for his insecurities, which were confided tightly and securely in a wrath of rage and contempt he had for the entire world. He demanded constant reassurance and surrounded himself with people too afraid not to give it to him. As I got older, it became more and more clear that he was nothing more than a scared, weak man whose inability to exercise any emotional regulation exploded into full-blown temper tantrums when he was triggered.

To this day, I still sometimes feel random butterflies of anxiety in my stomach on Sundays. Nothing good ever happened on Sundays.

Sundays involved church and transitioning back to my mom's house after having spent the weekend with Dad.

The anxiety of returning to Mom's house involved never knowing what I was returning home to. Would Mom have new bruises? Would there be a horrible, deafening, unspoken tension in the room that made me walk on eggshells? Did they find something in my room? I never knew. Each home had its own version of atrocities. They were very different and required different levels of alertness for survival.

That's not to say there were never good times at either house. There were, and despite their parenting and what they allowed us to be exposed to, I still loved them and wanted more than anything to please them and make them proud of me, not of my accomplishments, but of ME. I don't think I ever really accomplished that. Luckily, that became less important as I learned to be proud of myself.

I think many factors led me to becoming a psychotherapist. Trying to understand my parents, their choices, and my family are definitely at the top of that list. I don't think either of my parents ever truly understood the unchanging impact that one emotionally abusive event can have on a child's mind, even if that event is surrounded by ten other nurturing and functional ones. It doesn't change the bad. One drop of gasoline in a glass of milk may not kill you but it will make the milk taste like shit.

Chapter Eight
The Average Kid

I was a smart and inquisitive student, just not in the conventional sense. I had no idea I was smart at the time, however. I found school to be difficult. Aside from a couple of courses that came naturally, I struggled.

Looking back, I probably would have qualified for an IEP. I struggled with reading comprehension and math. I still do. It took me longer to learn things. Because of this, I never found myself in any college prep courses. My academic experience took place in general ed classes. Instead of algebra or trig, I took classes like applied mathematics. It gave me the math credits I needed to graduate but neither the experience nor the confidence. This fact brought me to a conclusion that I would struggle with for most of my life: I simply wasn't that bright. I carried myself as if I were smart. I kept company that would imply I felt good about myself, but I never really did.

In 10th grade, my classmates started talking earnestly about college and what to do after high school. Sure, there had been light-hearted comments about this or that friend wanting to attend such and such college when they grew up, but in my sophomore year, the talk became serious. People were starting to make actual plans.

That year, I heard all kinds of students talking about college: smart kids, average kids, all of them. I remember feeling tempted by moments of curiosity, enticed by the idea that perhaps I could go to college, too. I excelled in the arts, as well as English and Spanish. Languages came easily to me. Perhaps there was a place for me.

I still remember the day. I had picked up some brochures in the guidance counselor's office on a couple of different colleges and a schedule for the SAT exam. I thumbed through them with sweaty palms, looking at the pictures and imagining myself in them. Would I live in a dorm? Would I make friends? The questions were swimming in my head.

"Breathe. Just breathe." I told myself.

After many rehearsed conversations, I decided how I would bring up the topic with my parents.

"Oh, I picked these up at school today," I casually tossed the brochures on the table.

My stomach still tightens just thinking about that moment all these years later.

I don't recall the exact words. I just know what came after. I believe it was a brush-off of sorts; something similar to "Oh, ok."

But the conversation that night still rings in my ears to this day.

"Look, you are just an average kid, and that's fine. Don't try to be something you're not. You are no better than any of us. Besides, you are going to feel so bad about yourself when you fail (not if, but when), and we just don't want to see you so disappointed."

And the final bullet to put me out of my misery...

"Even if you did try to go to one of these schools, it's something your dad would have to pay for. There's no way we could pay for something like that."

I felt my ears get hot with shame and embarrassment. I had stepped out of line. The real tragedy was that it didn't anger me. It didn't make me act out in an argument or defiance. It should have, but it didn't because I believed what they said was true.

I am reminded of a similar event when I was 12.

I had it in my head that I wanted to be, and that I could, in fact be, an artist. I loved to draw — the shading, the contouring, the textures, manipulating the eye to see added dimensions simply by the way the pencil touched the paper. It was like magic.

It was in that house, running across those black patterns in the carpet to show my dad. "Look! Look what I drew!" Pine trees outlining a lake, complete with shadows and ripples on the water. I was so proud. I waited for that moment of pride to come across his face as well, hoping he would see my talent and encourage me. Where I hoped for acknowledgment, I found dismissal. "An artist, huh? Um... what else do you want to be when you grow up?"

He must have seen the pain in my face because he followed up with what I can only assume he thought was reassurance, an explanation, or perhaps brutal honesty.

"What I mean is, if you were going to be really good, you would be by now. Take that kid, Adam, at church. He's your age. Have you seen some of the stuff that kid can draw? It's like looking at a photograph!"

The words stung. It never occurred to me that I was not good. But now I knew. They had solidified what I knew in my gut to be true: I wasn't good enough. I wasn't smart enough, and any fantasy I had to the contrary was something I needed to squash now before it became a problem. I took every thought I had allowed myself to think, every dream, every what if, and buried it so deep I could deny it ever existed. I wasn't an artist, and I wasn't college material. All I could see were the things I couldn't be. I hoped that maybe by default, what I could be would start to become clear.

Fast-forward to 1987. As my senior year drew to a close, I found myself still grappling with the question of what came next, armed with nothing but a clear understanding of everything I wasn't good at.

"So what ARE you going to do after high school?"

The question wasn't asked outright, but it was there. I had been expected to have a job since I was in 8th grade, if I ever wanted any money for anything at all. While other kids enjoyed their summers, my mom had gotten me a job with the school district, painting classrooms and cutting grass. Other odd jobs followed as the seasons changed. The jobs I had were important ones, and to this day, I value people in our communities who do them, but for me, it was mind-numbing .

Chapter Nine
A Cultural Shift

In high school, I discovered that I had a passion for language arts, in particular, the Spanish language. There were often several exchange students at our school from around the world. It fascinated me. I found the different cultures, languages, and ideas of normality to be provocative and exciting. I had been raised with a rigid and definitive sense of things in life being categorically right or wrong. There was no grey area. In befriending exchange students from cultures different than my own and learning more about those cultures, I was discovering that, in fact, the world was made up of grey areas. Right and wrong, as I had come to understand those words, were very much relative, in my evolving opinion.

I had several meaningful friendships with students from other countries. I decided that I wanted a closer experience with what it was like to be transplanted temporarily, but I lacked the confidence to be an exchange student myself.

Having done some minimal research, I approached my father about the idea of having an exchange student in our home. I never would have guessed he would have agreed to the idea, but he did. This was entirely out of character for him, and I would not have predicted it.

We got connected with an organization called AFS. We had some family interviews, and late in my junior year, my family was matched with a boy from Bolivia who was to arrive in the coming school year. I was thrilled to have this experience .

I had a small, close circle of friends with whom I could relate. They were all in the choir or drama club. I found the show choir to be a safe haven and a place where I excelled.

Talking to my friend Michele had always been effortless. She also lived just a few blocks from me, so spending time together was easy. She had an infectious sense of humor. She was fun to hang out with. I loved that her eyes disappeared when she laughed. Michele was a caring and compassionate friend. She gave her all in her friendships. She had an unyielding loyalty to those she loved.

Unfortunately, that also came with a pretty strong judgment. She was quick to point out bullshit and in most cases that fit well in my friendship with her. She was what I needed at the time.

I trusted her with everything in me.

Michele's family had been known as the Kool-Aid house in our neighborhood because it was where all our friends met. It was close, so it was typically the gathering spot either for a game of cards on the weekends or after a choir concert. Her mom and stepdad, Dee and Al, had become surrogate parents for many of us. The fact that they let us drink and smoke at their house was also a major plus, though. They were the cool parents most of us didn't have. It's not that they didn't have their own family dysfunction. I'm sure they did, we just rarely saw it. It was refreshing. My parents had few issues with my friends but my house was far too rigid for my home to ever be a hangout spot for any of us.

Of everyone, my folks liked Michele best. She was the kind of friend parents trusted. It's not that she never did anything; she just never got caught.

She used to boast, "Parents love me."

She was right, and it worked. If I ever wanted permission to do anything of questionable morality, aka fun, all I had to do was say I was going with Michele or that she was going to be present, and that usually got me the green light.

I must have had a similar effect on her mom because I was one of the only teen boys allowed to hang out with Michele in her bedroom.

I think one of the things I liked best about my group of friends is that I don't think I ever officially came out to any of them. I didn't have to. It wasn't because I was overtly flamboyant or obvious necessarily, but rather that it was just kind of known and, therefore, a non-issue. You can't ask for friends better than that.

Michele also knew my parents well. She knew my obstacles. I was not out to my parents on any level; she sometimes helped me navigate that.

My junior year was the point in time when I stopped sharing how bad things were at home with friends. I had become sexually active and had embraced my attraction to other guys. Looking back, I never really had a plan per se to ever come out to my parents, but rather a plan to keep it from them indefinitely. I categorically chose not to think about how impossible that would be in the long term.

Chapter Ten
The Outing

Like most guys my age, my 17-year-old hormones did most of my thinking for me. I had grown accustomed to coupling that with navigating the mine field of my parents' rules, bigotries, and expectations. My father's house was the facade of family Christian values. My mother's house was the epitome of racist domestic violence rhetoric. I knew the rules of each household. I knew them well. I had to.

It was tough to find the space in between those two environments for casual gay teen exploration, but luckily, I was rarely on anyone's radar. Unless I spoke up, no one noticed me. My younger sister, however, was very much on their radar. She was 5 years younger than me. For whatever reason she was bad at lying, good at making poor choices and rarely learned from the consequences of those bad choices. She was in trouble frequently.

Whenever I got in trouble, I stored that mistake away in my mind, like a steel trap. I never got in trouble for the same thing twice. My sister lived for the moment and didn't do nearly the strategic planning I did. I never intentionally used that to my advantage, and I hated that she got in trouble more than I did. She stayed on their radar. The younger years were more traumatic, especially for my sister, I think. I remember the hitting. I remember the screams. When it came to my sister, my mom didn't know how to stop hitting once she started. Be it a belt or a ping pong paddle, the screams and yelling still rent space in my head. No matter where I hid in the house, I couldn't block out the sound of my sister's screams.

My mother's mother had done the same to her. Even as a child, understanding the reasons and the cycle never made it any less terrifying.

However, there was a distinct moment in time when my parents' attention shifted back towards me. It was the 1980s.

It would be many years before teens had advanced technology that provide more privacy. All we had was passing notes, writing things on paper, or talking on the phone. The obvious danger, of course, with note writing or journaling was that anyone could read it.

I still remember my teacher in high school, Ms. Newcomb, who once told us,

"Think twice about putting anything in writing that you don't want others to know."

She was right about that.

My parents had suspected I was gay for a while. They didn't approach me directly or put it into words, but it was what made my father steal a letter I had placed in the mailbox to be mailed to a guy I had been sneaking to see on occasion. In the letter were explicit details of sexual encounters. There was no hiding it.

I came home that day to find my father sitting at the table waiting for me. He was silent, expressionless, and pale.

"Sit down. We need to talk."

He was stern. He wasn't joking. My father didn't really ever raise his voice at us, but that day he began to yell, and it scared me. I'll never forget it.

"What the hell is this shit!?" He threw the letter he had stolen and opened without my permission onto the table.

I froze. There was nothing I could say that would benefit this situation, so I said nothing.

He continued.

"You don't give a fuck about anybody but yourself! Thanks to you, I had to go spend $70 today that I didn't have just to talk to a therapist and keep myself from jumping off of a goddamn roof and killing myself after I read this fucking trash! You're sick!"

I was seething, but I said nothing. I knew all about my father's affairs with other women my whole life. I knew what a hypocrite he was from Monday through Saturday, then on Sunday, he walked into that church every week pretending to be someone he wasn't, and now he was looking down his nose at me? Fucking asshole. Still, I said nothing. I just took it. He continued.

"And what about this boy coming from Bolivia? We have to fix this before he gets here! What if people at AFS find out?! Do you have any idea how this makes our family look?!"

My stepmother was also sitting at the table. She was a meek woman. Soft spoken. I had never in my life heard her so much as say the word crap without a giggle, let alone swear. She always pretended to be wholesome. It was nauseating. Like my father, that was also an act. Her role was to be the submissive Christian wife, and she played it to the hilt.

She sat there looking at me with her sad puppy dog eyes as if she were 8 years old and someone had just thrown away her ice cream. She disapproved, and this is how she expressed it. She made me sick. She was holier than thou, and raising her voice simply wouldn't be "a very

Christian thing to do," so she never did.

Her sickening submissiveness made me speak up. I turned my attention to her during one of my father's pauses in his rant. In the most sarcastic tone I could muster,

"Well," I said to her "Don't just sit there. Let's do this. What's your verdict? By all means, don't hold back."

I resented her pitiful stare. It was patronizing.

I was inviting her to the fight because I knew she wouldn't. It was safe. I didn't give a shit what her verdict was. I was just tired of listening to my dad. It was scaring me. Directing my mounting frustration towards her was a good distraction for me and Dad both.

As she began to speak, she tilted her head in a passive condescending way and said in a whispery voice, "We are so concerned for you. This is not a righteous path, and your dad and I are both worried about your soul."

Yes, she actually said that!

I rolled my eyes. Jesus fucking Christ, could she BE more self righteous?! I said nothing back to her because she sickened me to the extent I couldn't find the words. I never had an ounce of respect for her, and this was why. Clearly, I was a kid in her home who was going through something, who was struggling. She could have tried to connect with me in many ways, but what did she do? She judged me. It's all she knew, ironically. One of the many reasons I detest Christianity or at least the version of it that I experienced.

I recall that conversation word for word, but I have no memory of what my punishment was, aside from having one mandatory session with a Christian therapist. I stand by the fact that faith-driven therapy is such a crock. Faith, as I experienced it, was nothing but judgment. Therapy, as I understand it, is all about a space void of judgment. I still have no idea why people insist on combining the two. I remember that incident. It exists in a bubble in my mind.

I do recall that my father had called my mother and told her about the letter. My mother and her husband had a different approach to dealing with my deviance.

They had time to prepare their strategy. They calculated for maximum effect. My stepfather chose this time not to lose his shit and break things. He was creepily calm. He also chose not to scream and yell. What they said to me was much louder than screaming. It went something like this:

"If this is who you are, you need to tell us now. Tell us now so we can go ahead and get you written out of the will, (which was funny because they didn't have shit) and kicked out of this house.

My mother added, "If we see you on the street, we won't turn our heads to spit in your direction." It was a threat.

My mother actually said that. As long as I live and through all the good times we had in our relationship, she never once apologized for having said that. As the years passed, she just pretended she had never said it, but she said it pretty clearly that day.

No one was yelling. They were informing me, giving me information. I sat in silence, terrified it was about to get violent. They weren't done.

"And I hope you get some good life insurance because all queers get AIDS. Everyone knows that."

Mom had never been the aggressor. She was often powerless to stop her husband from abusing me, but I'd never gotten this from her directly, and it chilled me to the bone.

My memory stops there. That, too, exists in a bubble in my mind, even though I can repeat the dialogue verbatim. That day my parents told me that being a part of the family was very much conditional.

Again, I have no memory of a punishment. I think the intervention alone was the punishment. I was humiliated, violated, and completely stripped of any self-respect. Is this how they had wanted me to feel?

Being a parent now, I cannot, in any parallel universe, imagine saying things like that to my child. You could hold a gun to my head, and my life would end there because nothing in the universe would ever allow me to speak words like that to my child; nothing.

I do not recall my exact words, but I remember the message. They were giving me an out. They were giving me the opportunity to lie to them and say I wasn't really gay. They were giving me the opportunity to just stop doing it.

Want to know the worst part? I wasn't as angry as I had been with my father. I believed them. I thought myself to be so selfish as to hurt them like that. What was I thinking?

I had disappointed them, which was worse than any punch or punishment. I didn't want to get AIDS, and I didn't want to be homeless. I was in no position to lose my family. Abusive as they were, they were all I knew, and I loved them. Even after my mom had just said those horrific things to me moments before. I had always seen her as the victim of her husband. She had never protected us from him; and she didn't now, either. Still, I saw what I had done had hurt her and I regretted it.

I wanted desperately for things to go back the way they were before they knew. I hated the way they looked at me now. I hated that they no longer trusted me. They looked at me as something dirty, something shameful.

Nothing more was said about the topic and I would spend years compensating to win back their love and trust. My resolve was that if I just stopped sucking dick then that means I am not gay. I truly believed that.

Chapter 11
The Invitation

I slowly drifted off my parents' radar as the year progressed. It was my senior year. Eloy Avila had arrived from Bolivia and had integrated well into my social circle and into my family. Eloy was a delightful, charming boy. He was also exactly the distraction my family, on both sides, needed. The fighting, the danger, and the screaming seemed frozen in time now. None of us had forgotten, but maybe we could all have a good relationship with one another?

Eloy was in our home now. He shared a room with me. Things were drastically different. I had a brother, and it was nice. I had a real brother.

I still had the occasional sexual fling with a random gay kid from my school, but it was much more difficult. With each stolen kiss, each sexual meeting, I'd tell myself it was the last time. It was the last time, each time.

I don't think I ever told my friends not to tell Eloy, or maybe I did. I don't remember. I think they just knew not to. I was trying to be good now.

Eloy and I had a relationship that I valued. It was conditional, not entirely honest, but I valued it because I was so intrigued by his culture...by someone so different from me. He had come from South America into our home. All the tension that was there prior was now covered under the blanket of what Eloy brought to our family. He was new. He was exciting. He helped me with my Spanish. I helped him with his English. I felt needed and significant.

The gay part of my life was something that simply no longer fit in any kind of conscious way, and I was okay with that because it brought me nothing but trouble. The hormonal part of my sexual urges was just something I took care of in private. Even though I had the occasional isolated slip-up, I still believed that one day I could just stop; after all, this was not who I really was. There was no way I was going to allow my past to ruin this relationship I had with my Bolivian brother. It was my biggest fear at the time. I kept the secret at all costs.

Eloy was with us for a year. In some ways, the year was a blink. In others, it was a lifetime, as if he had always been with us. I couldn't imagine a life without him in it. I felt a sickening panic in the pit of my stomach knowing his return to Bolivia was quickly approaching.

I shared many private thoughts and conversations with Eloy, all platonic but nonetheless precious. I had grown up with the ghost of my biological brother. I often wondered if he and I would be close. Then Eloy came into our lives, and it was like a gift from the universe. I learned what it could be to have a brother, and I also learned about a world that existed outside the boundaries of Englewood, Ohio.

Midway through Eloy's year with us, during one of our late-night talks, I heard him ask from the bottom bunk, "Hey, why don't you come home with me?"

I was certain I'd misheard him. "What?" I sat up in bed.

"Yeah, why don't you come home with me? When I go back to Bolivia, come with me. I'll talk to my parents. You can have your own room,

58

and I'll show you around Trinidad. Stay as long as you want. I know my parents would love to meet you!" His family was extraordinarily grateful for our opening our home to Eloy, and they were equally gracious in return.

The rest of that senior year, I spent saving every dollar I earned. I did whatever I could to earn money, even if it meant spending less time with Eloy. I mean, when would I ever get this opportunity again?

I was stunned when my parents gave me permission to go. I think they knew that as long as I paid for it myself, they couldn't really stop me. By the end of the year, I had enough money saved for a six-month stay and a round-trip ticket.

My parents' only real question or concern was, "Why do you want to do this? What if his country is dangerous? Why would you want to leave home?"

I had always been taught that the world was an unsafe place. Exploring things outside my culture was not something people in my family did. Not to say that it was forbidden, but I don't think it ever crossed anyone's mind to encourage it. The world simply didn't really exist outside Ohio in any kind of real or safe way.

Eloy was scheduled to leave in August, and my ticket to Bolivia wasn't until September. Saying goodbye to him was heartbreaking. Yes, I would see him in a month, but the dynamic he brought to my family, the brotherly bond we had here, all of that was coming to an end, and I was devastated.

I watched my parents, my friends, and my siblings say goodbye to him that last day. We all ugly-cried, snot and all. They would never see him again, and I think we all knew it.

Chapter Twelve
Bolivia

I t was not until I sat down in the airline seat that I realized I was scared to death to fly. I was alone. I had never flown in an airplane before, and I was flying. By myself, to fucking Bolivia!! I was as thrilled as I was scared. A world I had only heard stories about existed somewhere on the other side of this flight. This plane was taking me directly to it and away from everything else.

Once the plane was in the air, my anxiety about flying vanished. This was amazing! There was even a smoking section in the back of the plane! I could smoke, and my parents would never know! Ha! This was amazing! I flew from Dayton to Miami, Florida, to Lima, Peru, then on to La Paz, Bolivia, where I was to meet Eloy and his friend Pablo.

I remember getting off the plane in La Paz. I was overstimulated and simply couldn't respond to anything anymore. I was exhausted but filled with anticipation to see my brother again. I searched for his face in the crowds of people gathered in the terminal. Within a moment, I heard him call my name. There he was! He had climbed up on a stairwell and was holding onto a wooden pillar for balance so he could lean over and see me above the crowd. God, I missed that face! I missed our late-night talks. I missed all of it. I missed him.

Eloy lived in a tiny village called Trinidad. Back then, there were no roads connecting the capital city of La Paz to Trinidad, and the only way to travel between them was by plane. The plane we took from La Paz to Trinidad was one of those tiny planes that allowed you to feel every breeze and wind gust. With every wobble and shimmy, I was convinced that I was going to go the way of Buddy Holly and the Big Bopper.

I have no idea what it is like today, but Trinidad, as I experienced it in 1987, was a tropical, unassuming paradise in many respects. The people were some of the most genuine, humble people I had ever met. Located in the jungle, Trinidad is surrounded by lagoons and tributaries. The roads were all dirt, and the main method of transportation around the area was by motorcycle or scooter.

Being one of only two landlocked countries in South America, Bolivia is also one of the poorest. I knew poverty. I thought I knew poverty. I didn't know poverty. Poor plumbing, primitive drainage, and sewer conditions showed me how fortunate I had been in the States. The poverty and poor living conditions of some of the residents only added intrigue for me. The people in Trinidad fell much closer to either end of the poverty spectrum, with few people in the middle.

Eloy's parents lived in a huge two-story white stucco house. The cool ceramic tiles on the floors and walls kept the temperate air calm inside, away from the blistering heat. There was no AC. Even in nice houses, like Eloy's, geckos ran across the ceilings and walls. They were, I learned, welcome visitors since their diet consisted of mosquitoes and small insects.

Eloy's parents treated me like a prince. They were the most gracious and thankful adults I had ever met. Eloy's mother, Olga, spoke no English. None. His father, Teddy, could speak some broken English at best. Olga was a full-time housewife. With the help of their maid, she spent her days cleaning, dusting, and cooking. That was her life. She did all of it with love and enthusiasm daily, seemingly without rest.

Nothing about this environment was anything I knew. It was nothing I expected and so much more than I could have hoped for. It was completely foreign in every way. I had no idea my soul needed that. Bolivia and the friends I would make there changed my life in ways I'm still not sure I deserved.

Since I was 12, I had always had to work. I didn't even realize that I didn't know how to relax. I didn't know the joy of driving a motorcycle around the plaza in a loop, just honking at friends and waving. The central plaza was a primary social area surrounded by small local merchants and vendors.

Occasionally, I noticed quite social sloths lazily hanging out in the palm trees that surrounded the plaza. Their large, clumpy bodies reaching for that next branch were so painfully slow, as if they never had anywhere to be for any reason whatsoever. I couldn't imagine.

I often heard Capuchin monkeys chattering and jumping from limb to limb over the passersby in the streets. In contrast to the poor sloths, the monkeys always had somewhere to be and were always late getting there.

In my experience, animals have been more trustworthy than humans. I tend to notice them in my environment. To some people, animals may be a background feature in an environment. To me, they were often the first thing I noticed.

I was so distracted by my new environment that I didn't immediately notice my relationship with Eloy had taken a significant shift. He was distant, more solitary. He was not unkind at all, and there had been no conflict, but I noticed that after he had shown me around town, introduced me to his parents and a few friends and relatives, he had created some distance between us. It was not even awkward; he just didn't need me in the way he had when we were in the States.

Furthermore, it became quite evident that the friends I had made on my own in those first few months were mine alone. Eloy knew my friends, but he and I definitely ran in different social circles. It surprised me that I was not offended or hurt, but I wasn't. I was too busy. I was the monkey.

Eloy's family, gracious as they were, were also people who were not subtle about their class. Teddy had a small plane, and he would fly the family out periodically for outings in the country outside the jungle. Money was simply a non-issue because they always had plenty of it.

My friends, however, did not share this convenience. Although they were certainly not like some of the people I had seen outside of town living in huts with tarps and dirt floors, they were more middle-class with humble roots and a passion for life and its simplicities that I found intoxicating.

I have no memory of how I met these people as funny as that may sound. They were just there. They were people I encountered in my outings and talking with locals.

One of my first male friends was Iver Pedraza. He was a handsome boy about my age. He had a soft round baby face with a smooth adolescent complexion. He was small in stature with dark brown hair and a warm, welcoming smile. He was one of my first friends. We took walks in the plaza, rode motorcycles in town, and went piranha fishing in the lagoons.

Iver was genuine and sweet. Looking back, I think he and I must have had countless conversations where we each lacked the vocabulary to understand every word. Miraculously this did not diminish the quality of those conversations. I invited him for lunch to Eloy's house on a few occasions, and I enjoyed my friendship with Iver so much. Iver's innocent, youthful expressions made it hard for me to imagine him ever disappointing his parents the way I had mine.

I also met a girl named Karen. She and her sisters, Cinthia and Patty, became people whom I visited daily sometimes. Karen had a remarkable talent for speaking English. Few people in the town had mastered it, but even at that young age, she had, and I was always impressed by that.

My friends and the people I met in general were so different from any Americans I had encountered. Even strangers would meet me with the most honest and precise intentions—kindness and affection. It was distinct and observable.

As a young gay 19-year-old boy, I recall feeling gleefully confused that it was common for heterosexual teen boys to walk around town with their arms around their friends' shoulders as they chatted. Affection and human contact were not only socially acceptable, but it was considered rude if you didn't engage in it. It made the American culture I knew feel cold and distant. I carried a great envy and regret that I had never known this culture.

I experienced many drunken hug-filled nights with many friends. Bonfires, social gatherings, and visits were all part of how I spent my time with these new families I had found.

Some of the cultural traditions were smothered in notions of romantic overture. I witnessed young boys and men gathering their friends and their guitars (because most people played the guitar) and meeting at young girls' houses at night to serenade them.

Gathering at a friend's house on some random night to have a group sing-along was commonplace. American music was popular, and the boys would learn these songs on their guitars. However, since English was not common, most of my friends could not sing them. I recall one gathering with friends where they played "Yesterday" by the Beatles.

The voices in the room fell to a hushed whisper when I started belting out the lyrics one drunken night. The guitars were my backup, and I sang for my friends that night. I remember my friend Sagmar whispering to his friend "Shh...quiero escuchar. Él realmente puede cantar!" (I want to listen. He can really sing.)

My confidence that night was only matched when months later, I learned to master the lyrics of "Eclipse total del amor" ("Total Eclipse of the Heart" by Bonnie Tyler) THEN, I knew I was the shit! I mean, who knew the Spanish word for "powder keg"? That's right! This guy! I was proud.

I recall the formalities and elegance of the quinceañeras when a teenage girl would turn 15. This was her transition into official womanhood and it was held in the upmost of regard and respect.

Marcelo was a friend of Karen. He was a beautiful breath of fresh air. He was larger than most of my friends and much more flamboyant. Im not sure if he knew he was gay back then, but we all did. Marcelo used to talk to me about how much he loved the cities and how he loved the idea of walking around in a fashionable warm clothes in the cold smoking a cigarette. He spoke of how someday he'd do that. He was right. Today, Marcello is a sucessful celebrity fashion designer with his own televison show.

Leaving Bolivia was more painful and sorrowful than any departure I had experienced. Leaving the people I had come to know and love felt like such a betrayal, a betrayal to them and to myself.

Karen, Iver, Sagmar, all of them were not just friends. They were fragments of my new self. Fantasies of returning and even of staying flooded my mind. I had grown and changed in ways I hadn't expected. I was not at all the same person I was when I arrived. A door had been opened in my heart that would be impossible to close. I had to walk through it.

Chapter Thirteen
Вы говорите по-русски?

I tried with urgency to articulate to people back in Ohio what I had experienced in South America. I tried to talk about the life-changing events and how I felt so different, but nothing translated. It all only existed in some other place. It was like trying to describe colors to a blind person.

I spoke on the phone with my friends from Bolivia, and we wrote letters back and forth. This was still many years before anyone even heard the words cell phone or internet. Any contact I had with that world was arduous. In some respects, the contact almost made it more painful to reacclimate. After a few phone bills, calls to Bolivia became shorter and less frequent as I could not pay for the hundreds of dollars in charges.

Now that I was back in the States, I had no purpose. I had graduated from high school and was working menial jobs. My closest friend was off at college. Michele had gone to Bowling Green University. I had no one. All the passion for life I found in Bolivia was now sucked from my soul and little was left. I had become a surplus to my own life. No one needed me to be or to do anything.

One day as I grabbed an old duffle bag that had been tossed into the back of my closet a brochure fell out. I picked it up and began reading again. It was for the US Navy. I had grabbed it from school over a year ago, before Bolivia. Was this really my only option? Dread. Nothing but dread.

I read about the GI bill, the VA loans, and all the benefits—things my family could never provide for me. It was all right there, for the taking. More importantly, though, I would make them proud. That fact was bigger and more important than anything I ever wanted for myself. I was painfully aware that my only focus was on what the military could do for me instead of what I wanted to do. I felt no sense of honor or purpose or even an idea of what kind of job I would do once I was in.

I couldn't go to college. I couldn't cut grass for the rest of my life. What choice did I have? Bolivia had left me with a sense of obligation to live. An obligation for nobility and passion. Where the fuck was that? It certainly wasn't here. The air in Ohio had become far too still for me. In that stillness was nothingness.

There was something else nagging me. What about the gay thing? I never allowed myself to think these words consciously. It was far too scary to admit. I stuffed it down. Move on—nothing to see here.

Reluctantly, I made an appointment with a recruiter.

I went to the recruiting office downtown on a Saturday. Very few memories remain in my head about the conversations I had with him or the details, just something about a test called an ASVAB (armed services vocational aptitude battery) exam to see in what areas I might excel. As nervous as I was, I was finally excited about this test! Finally! A tool to point me in a direction. Any direction, really, just a direction. I was still convinced I was too dumb to go to college, but knew I was too smart to do manual labor forever. I was lost. One of the facts I had gotten from the recruiter was that numerous jobs in the navy wouldn't necessarily put me in harm's way, even jobs that didn't involve being on a ship. This ASVAB exam could actually help me get somewhere.

Like other aptitude tests, this one did not require studying, and I was glad about that. I was never a good test taker in school, so having one that I couldn't fail was a relief. It simply measured what I knew and what my skills might be.

Test day came. There were several parts, including topics like science, math, reading, mechanics, etc. I can't tell you anything about any of those sections or how I did. One section sticks out to this day: language aptitude.

This is the part where you think I'm going to tell you that I breezed through that section, feeling good about myself, right? Nope. It was awful. I stumbled through it in a way I hadn't anticipated. That old familiar feeling of being stupid was alive and well.

Here were the directions: They give you a paragraph of text. The text, however, is written in a fictitious language. There were four or five grammar rules spelled out for this language. Based on those grammar rules, my job was to translate the paragraph into English. I remember thinking "What the fuck?! Seriously?"

Painstakingly, I fumbled through what I thought were the nouns, verbs, conjugations, and past participles. I felt a sense of panic as I desperately wished I'd paid more attention in class. Calm down. Panic isn't going to help. Just breathe.

Time expired, and I begrudgingly put down my pencil.

"Well, that sucked" I thought. Confident that I had found a way to fail an unfailable test, I went home defeated and discouraged.

I later discovered that most people who felt they did horribly on that part of the exam were the ones who did quite well, and vice versa. Unbelievably, at the time, my scores were high enough to qualify for one of the most prestigious language schools in the country: the Defense Language Institute in Monterey, California. I was to go into the Russian program to become a Russian linguist!

For a moment, I thought there had to be a mix-up. Surprisingly, after that initial moment, I completely allowed myself to believe it. I was going to California to be a Russian linguist! I felt as if NASA itself had walked into my general ed classes back in high school and told me I was chosen to be an astronaut!

Chapter Fourteen
Bootcamp

I am grateful for many things. One of these is the fact that my 18-year-old naivety allowed me to have no idea of the mind games and mental abuse of boot camp. It was hell. Looking back through a more educated lens, I totally get it. It's sick, but I get it. Bootcamp is designed to weed out independent thinkers and weak individuals and reprogram them to mindlessly take orders without questioning authority. If you're too educated or too strong-willed, they sometimes get you with the lie of nationalism. They strip you of any shred of individual self-worth and then attempt to mentally rebuild you as a collective. Within that collective, they brainwash you into feeling an undying sense of loyalty and unwavering dedication to the collective. This collective, of course, is your country. I understood patriotism for exactly what it was: taught hatred of anyone different than yourself.

I grew up in various kinds of abuse. I was no stranger to being screamed at, hit, or intimidated. This was much of the same.

It's a strange feeling to be treated as if you're stupid while simultaneously being too smart to buy into the rhetoric being taught. I remember being taught many inane things during my training.

Everything from how to fold a 45-degree angle on the corner of a bedsheet to pass inspection (because there is no other reason to do it), to how to put my own hand into my own goddamn pocket.

The company commander would stand in front of the troops and scream (because he screamed everything) instructions on how to place your hand in the pocket of your dungarees. He would put all his fingers together to form a paddle like shape then explain "Then you slide your hand into the pocket just like you're sliding it into a wet pussy." I wasn't offended by that because I'm gay. I was offended by it because I have a brain. Nearly everything this man would teach us, he somehow felt that comparing the task to a pussy would somehow resonate with us like no other instruction would. I mean, what is that? There were a handful of guys in my platoon who felt the same and who were as disgusted as I was by the ignorant display of misogynistic, knuckle-dragging instructions we were receiving on how to serve our country.

Daily, I had grown men standing an inch from my face, screaming at the top of their lungs "WHAT THE FUCK IS WRONG WITH YOU?!! YOU FUCKING DUMBASS!" My company commander would scream so close in my face, I would always get a whiff of halitosis mixed with breath mints.

Granted, this kind of attack was not the result of anything I had or hadn't done, simply my existence, and maybe a mistaken moment of eye contact was enough to spark such an attack. It didn't matter who you were. It was a show. It was meant to keep everyone afraid to question anything. To keep you hyper alert to jump at a moment's notice when someone screams. It was basically PTSD training. Fight or flight. Public humiliation = obedience.

I longed for the opportunity to get into my language school when boot camp was over. I wondered if it was ever going to happen. I kept telling myself this was worth it. The opportunities I was going to have were going to make all of this hell worthwhile.

Nearly half of our time was spent preparing for dress uniform inspections. You got dressed, stood in formation with your hands behind your back (parade rest), and waited for the inspector to walk by you, looking for any loose thread hanging from a seam. I could feel his hot breath in my face as he ran his calloused hands across my face to check for any hint of stubble.

During one such inspection, on a seemingly random day, I watched a 19-year-old boy end his own life right in front of me. We were standing in formation, which meant you were forbidden to move or speak. Out of my peripheral vision, I noticed someone standing on the roof of the building we were standing in front of. The building was no more than a few hundred feet away. I remember thinking to myself, "That's odd. I wonder what he's doing up there." Before I could even finish the thought, he was in the air. He dove towards the concrete below headfirst. In the following seconds, as we all gasped, I thought, "Someone had to help him! Someone had to make it stop! Someone had to stop all of this from happening! This should not be happening!" My mind was racing; the thoughts came fast and faster. Then he hit. It is a sound that will echo in my ears till the day I die. A terra-cotta pot full of dirt as it falls off a balcony and crashes onto the sidewalk. That's what it sounds like when a 19-year-old human skull shatters on the pavement. As long as I live, I'll never unhear that.

We were all just kids—none of us more than 20 years old. We all broke formation and scattered like panicked mice. We were quickly herded up and funneled back into our barracks. All remaining activities for the rest of the day were cancelled. The chaplain came to talk to us that evening. Until then, we were given the rest of the day off to calm down.

I was not at all religious at 20, but I was relieved to see that they were handling this suicide with some amount of responsibility by having the chaplain come around and debrief us. I guess they were human after all.

It was 8 p.m. when the chaplain finally arrived. He was a small Filipino man with a golden cross on his uniform to signify his job. He looked cold. He had no expression. Still, I was grateful he was there. For me, it was a sign that they not only acknowledged we had human emotions but that we were also allowed to process and express them.

As the chaplain stood before us, we all sat there on the cold linoleum floor waiting for his words of wisdom. I'm paraphrasing here, but his speech went something like this:

> What happened today was a tragedy. But we can learn something important. The fact of the matter is that kid was a coward! He's being sent home to his Mama in a box because he couldn't take it! It's better to know this now. He was weak! Can you imagine having someone onboard a ship like that as your shipmate to have your back!? We are better off without him.

My god. As I write these words, I still can't believe that happened. Aside from the sound of the chaplain's voice, the silence in the room was deafening. I just sat there - afraid to move, afraid to react. They were horrible, awful people.

Chapter Fifteen
Defensive Language Institute

Monterey is a place that immediately commands attention. The vastness of the Pacific stretches endlessly, its deep blue waters meeting rugged cliffs in a dramatic display. The hills and jagged cliffs overlooking beach scenes were so picturesque that I'd only seen it in movies. It was breathtaking. The fog loomed at the crest of the hills like it knew something and flowed around as it poured through the trees. The air carried a crisp, salty tang, refreshing and unmistakable. It was like nothing I had ever seen. I was actually here. This was finally real.

Walking along Cannery Row, I could almost hear echoes of Steinbeck's stories - the remnants of the old sardine industry now transformed into charming overpriced shops and seafood restaurants. The subtle stench of the sea lions as they barked lazily from the docks, utterly unbothered by the passing tourists. There was a raw beauty here, a perfect balance of history and nature, and I found myself drawn in, captivated.

At 20 years old, I arrived at the Defense Language Institute in Monterey, stepping into a world that felt both liberating and uncertain. After the rigid confines of boot camp, I was suddenly treated like an adult—few rules beyond curfew, the freedom to explore a mysterious new town. My dorm was a 3-story white brick building that was perched high on a fog-shrouded hill overlooking the scattered cottages below. The scene felt almost like summer camp, the excitement of possibility humming in the air.

Each day, I descended the steep path to those quaint little buildings, where the illusion of ease vanished. Inside, Russian class consumed us from 9 AM to 4 PM, an unrelenting storm of vocabulary, grammar, and immersion drills. The contrast was striking—serene on the outside, grueling within.

As a closeted gay man, I found myself balancing not just the intensity of the language, but the quiet weight of secrets I wasn't ready to share. The dorm was a hive of young male energy, a constant flow of bodies wrapped in nothing but small, white military-issued towels. The air was thick with something unspoken—lingering glances, fleeting smirks, the occasional brush of damp skin in the hallways. It was impossible to tell where the camaraderie ended and something more forbidden began. Maybe it was just the sheer relief of being free from boot camp, but sometimes the tension felt like something else, something fleeting, but never acknowledged.

The base was not just for the navy. There were linguist students here from the marines, air force and army as well. Each dorm was specific to that branch of service. I watched the people walk around on the sidewalks that climbed up the hills thoroughout the base. I felt so lucky and undeserving to be among them. In the back of my mind I still wondered how I had gotten here. I began to think more intensely about the mechanics of the Russian language.

I was surrounded by brilliant minds, people who were confident in their abilities. I often wondered—did I really belong here? I really had no desire to learn Russian whatsoever and quite frankly was still not entirely convinced that I could. As soon as I became aquatinted with someone of authority, I began the conversation of what steps I'd need to take to get transferred to the Spanish department. Afterall, I was freshly home from Bolivia and would have easily excelled.

If I could get transferred to the Spanish department. This experience would have been much more enjoyable I thought. I mean, my scores were high enough to get into this place, surely, I would be an asset in a language I already knew how to speak.

I learned many things in the military. One of those things was that decisions made by superior department heads sometimes held more aimless authoritarianism rather than logic. Transferring to the Spanish department was not an option for two reasons: the first was that the Spanish department was already allegedly over filled by 150%. The second reason was my score. The higher scores were automatically assigned to the more difficult languages like Russian, Czech and Farsi, while the lower scores were sent to languages like Spanish and French. I still couldn't help but think there was some sort of mistake with my test scores.

During orientation we were also told another little gem: DLI had a 90% fail rate. While most schools would be ashamed of this, DLI took pride in it. My heart sank. I had never worked well under that kind of pressure.

I remember feeling a chill thinking about all the money the military spent on getting all of us top-secret security clearance and background checks. How did it make sense to want a 10% success rate? I still can't answer that question.

All language classes were taught by native speakers from that country. My instructor was this tiny little Russian woman, I'd guess in her 40's. She smelled like sickening sweet grandma perfume and she seemed annoyed when any of us struggled with the course curriculum. She personalized it. She raised her voice in frustration each time any of us answered a question incorrectly. In the evenings we listened to hours of Russian cassettes and then were paired up with a classmate to practice. We worked feverishly on our written skills in the workbooks we had to take with us wherever we went.

The curriculum at DLI was in hyper drive and I was falling behind fast. The further behind I got the more accelerated the course work seemed. The Russian program was a year long. At the six-month mark, it became clear to me and everyone else that I was going to fall in the 90%. I tried everything, tutors, playing Russian cassettes in my sleep, extra studying. Nothing was working. I simply could not learn in this fast-paced setting. There was no room for error at all. I cried myself to sleep on many nights. I had a flash of being back in that applied mathematics class while my peers studied trigonometry.

The growing certainty that I would fail swirled around me and consumed me like the fog that rolled down the hill and filtered through the trees. I couldn't escape it. With it, came the old familiar message ringing louder in my ears:

I had stepped out of line and tried to be someone I wasn't.

I felt a self-induced humiliation that was like an emotional stench.

Before long, I was discharged from the language school, along with many of my peers. The fact that I was one of many who didn't make the cut did nothing to ease my depression. It felt cosmically unfair for the universe to have given me this opportunity only for me to fail. I felt defeated and humiliated. Any shred of self-esteem I had allowed myself to own was being peeled away like layers of an onion. It was raw and it hurt deeply.

What would I tell people? What would people think? The words of my parents still rang in my ears "You'll be so disappointed when you fail."

That's not to say they never encouraged me. They did. Particularly when I joined the military. Having a son in the military was a badge of honor for them. They had done something right.

It's just that the bad stuff from years earlier was much easier to believe and impossible to forget. My parents never apologized for their cruel words when I was in high school. They never attempted to address the damage they had done. To them, my joining the military and being accepted into this language school was proof that I had been scared straight.

In the navy, when you fail out of a school like that, they don't sit you down and say "Ok, what would you like to do now?" They didn't give a shit what I wanted. When you failed out of DLI, you had no individual value to the military.

Protocol was to ship any seamen who failed off to the fleet. I could have been assigned to any kind of ship big or small anywhere in the world. I had no control over it whatsoever. My destination was to do entry-level grunt work. Students who failed out of the school or who had any disciplinary action were all sent to the deck department to be boatswain mates.

The military mindset was to make the program as rigid as possible to only produce graduates who adapted to a specific way of learning. It took me many years to understand that I learn differently and struggle with test anxiety. It was even longer before I accepted that that had no bearing on my intelligence or ability to learn foreign languages. I just couldn't learn through rapid fire, even if it was in Monterey.

Chapter Sixteen
Don't Ask Don't Tell

A t this point I was trying desperately to hang on to the bragging rights that I had been accepted to a school like that at all. I was still trying to figure out the story of why I left. Because I still had security clearance I was assigned to a base in San Diego with nuclear submarines. I was stationed on the submarine tender U.S.S Dixon AS 37. Its mission was to repair and supply submarines.

One advantage of being stationed on a sub tender was they rarely went anywhere. One or two times a year we would go out to sea on short trips, but for most of the year we were tied to a dock. This meant that, if you could afford it, you could live in town and have some semblance of some normality. You just travel back and forth to the base as you would to a normal job. But most people lived on the ship, which was, if nothing else, a great way to save money.

The Dixon was home to roughly 2000 people, men and women. Although life on the ship was certainly not as hellish as bootcamp it was nothing like the prestige of the language School in Monterey. At DLI I shared a nice spacious room with a view with one other person. On the USS Dixon, I slept in a large room called a birthing area. About 400 of us

81

were each assigned a tiny twin sized mattress a few inches thick, called a rack. They were stacked three high on either side of narrow pathways that turned the room into a literal maze. There were more people on the boat than there were racks and so many beds were shared with someone who worked a different shift. Despite rigorous cleaning schedules, the birthing area consistently maintained a strong aroma of sweat, body odor, and just a hint of foot fungus.

I spent four years on that boat and subs. I met some amazing influential people. Some were fucking assholes and others made me a better person for having known them. One of the latter was Vinnie Hoffman.

Now, statistically speaking, on a ship of over 2,000 people there will be a significant LGBTQ population among them. We were present. Sometimes identifying other queer shipmates was easier than others.

Vinnie was one of those people who was easy to read even if your gaydar was a little rusty. Vinnie looked like she just walked off a rugby field. She had a solid frame of a body. Not overweight, just solid. She was also significantly taller than the average female sailor so she was not hard to spot in a crowd.

Vinnie had the body of a butch lesbian. No denying that. She took up space in a room in such a way that it made most cis het men uncomfortable, which was ironic because she was actually quite soft spoken and shy until she got to know you. I remember being so impressed that she changed her own oil in her car and knew when and how to replace spark plugs.

I have absolutely no idea how we met. Isn't that funny? No clue. I just remember that when we did first start talking it felt like I had made my first real true friend. We connected and that connection needed no real explanation. It simply was.

Vinnie was a sweet young woman and had a witty sense of humor.

She had an air of awkward goofiness in her humor that might make the average person think maybe she wasn't all that with it. The savage irony was she was one of those people who knew a little about just about everything. As I got to know Vinnie more and as our friendship grew, she was arguably one of the smartest, most brilliant people I have ever met and she felt absolutely no obligation to prove it to anyone.

She was my first connection to the gay world of San Diego. She lived off base with her girlfriend, Lee, who was also onboard our ship. I was instantly accepted into the small circle of lesbian friends Vinnie had introduced me to. Keep in mind this was all long before being gay was permitted in the military. We had to be careful. That was no joke. Yes we were fortunate to be stationed in a liberal state like California and even more fortunate to live off base among other gay folks, but once we were back on base all the rules changed and we all had to constantly remind ourselves of that.

It was 1990 and Bill Clinton had just began his "Don't ask don't tell" policy. The policy offered a minimal level of comfort to people who were signing up to join the military but for those of us already serving it was not helpful at all. LGBT folks had existed in the military since the conception of the armed forces. In fact, I would argue many of us are drawn to the military in disproportionate numbers due to escaping abusive homes and battling our own internalized homophobia.

I know that was the case for me. Joining the military was not only an alternative to college but was the most masculine thing I could think of. It gave me the sense I could lead a heteronormative life and it diverted away any unwanted suspicion to the contrary. It had not been a conscious awareness at the time, but in retrospect I can clearly see that I thought if I could just stop having sex with men then I wouldn't be gay. I could make my parents proud. I could be the son they wanted and deserved. The world Vinnie would show me would challenge all of that.

Vinnie and Lee took me to my first gay pride parade, introduced me to queer classics like "Torch Song Trilogy," and educated me about the historic significance of the Stonewall riots in the late 6os.

I still remember that first pride parade. I saw people from all walks of life, of all races, religions, organizations. There were couples and families. No demographic was unrepresented. I was in shock. The feather boas, the elaborate costumes - it was like a million craft stores had exploded onto the crowd filled streets. Tens of thousands of people cheering and celebrating, taking up as much emotional space as they could.

The music blasting from passing floats and the bass of the drumbeats vibrated in my chest. It also vibrated in my soul.

I felt the beat of a song I had never heard before. There was a moment. A moment when the sound all around me felt muffled, just for a moment, as if I had put on headphones. In that moment I heard the thought:

"Oh my God. What if...what if ...I'm okay?? What If I am even normal and all of this... is really ok?"

The very thought flew in the face of everything I had been taught and everything I thought I knew to be true. The version of myself in high school that I allowed to be some kind of gay only existed in safe corners of the school, in choir concerts and drama clubs and occasionally a secretive kiss. The knowledge existed among my circle of close friends. It existed in the passing of notes during class, but THIS? Never did I assume nor understand living like this; out in the open, unashamed. My brain never even knew it was possible to dream it.

I think one of the reasons it had been so impossible for me to decide what I wanted to do after high school was because I couldn't see a future where I'd be allowed to exist and take up space, not in any real or public way. The part of me that had allowed myself to enjoy those secretive kisses or affectionate hand holding among mutual friends only existed because I hid a tiny lie in the back of my brain that said one day I can just stop. If the day came that I could stop doing these things then that meant that same day would also hold acceptance from my family. The idea that the word gay was a part of my being was the furthest thing from my perception. It never occurred to me.

Now here I was, standing in the street among thousands of people who believe and were celebrating that very thing. They shared apartments and houses with friends and partners. They held jobs. They paid bills. They lived totally open lives, unapologetically, not seeking or needing anyone's permission. They just existed. You could have knocked me over with a feather boa.

As I learned more about queer culture, I realized, painstakingly, that my life had now become considerably more complicated. The thought of ever going back home at the end of my enlistment...was it even possible? Did I even want to? Where was home really?

I didn't have the answers to these questions. I did know one thing though. I wasn't going to allow myself to spend too much time consciously thinking about it. I was going to enjoy this freedom here in California as long as it lasted. What would happen post California was a problem for future Daniel. I lived in the moment and had fun doing it.

Having gay friends on the ship as well as civilians in the community gave me a sense of belonging and normality. For the first time, I found community. This community was a direct contrast to the life I had when I went back to that grey ship tied up to that pier every day. The United States military still owned me. I was about to understand the dangers of forgetting that.

This new freedom I had allowed myself to embrace was intoxicating! I was the preverbal kid in a candy store. I was young. I was thin and unbeknownst to me, apparently found to be quite attractive by a guy or two. Okay maybe a few more than one or two. Okay maybe a lot more.

I did stupid dangerous things. Picking up guys in Balboa park after dark, picking up guys at gay bars from different ports my ship visited. It was a blast! I had heard of the dangers of picking up guys in parks. Every once in a while someone would get murdered or gay bashed. I knew of it, but I also knew I had never felt this kind of freedom before. It was not just sex. It was the thrill of finding another gay guy to share that exciting forbidden sexual energy with. It was a public way of unapologetically taking up space. It was being myself. Any aspect of anonymity or risk only added to the excitement.

Because of the large population of gay people on the ship, it became easy to find gay groups of people to hang out with. It was also an environment where it was easy to bond with people and become friends, gay or not due to being confined in a small space.

Most people had their opinions on who was gay and who wasn't. I don't think there was anyone who was unaware we existed. That was a huge down side of DADT. We no longer hid in the shadows. People could see us. For the most part though, people would leave us alone.

People naturally gathered as they attracted like minds within their social circles. Northmont high school had social groups mainly consisting of jocks, nerds, and choir and band geeks. These same groups were just a little bit older and now carried titles like scuba divers, navigation specialist, engineers and deck hands.

Much like in high school, I was friends with all different kinds of people. I, of course, had my gay friends like Vinnie and Lee but I also had friends like Dan from the deck department. He had also found himself on the USS Dixon after an unsuccessful stint on a submarine. No one planned to work in the deck department. It was the default for everything else. It's where they sent you when you failed or lost your rank due to disciplinary action.

One of my first like-minded friends was Dan. Dan was my age, tall, a bit overweight and had this meaty face with cheeks a I imagine a grandmother would pinch. Dan was also highly intelligent, and I think, felt as out of place and as grossed out by that greasy cesspool of misogyny, as I was. I think in environments like that you either conform because you're one of them or you pool together like drops of oil in water. Dan was a fellow drop of oil.

He had a mischievous wicked antiestablishment side I loved and found intoxicating. He loved dungeons and dragons and listening to Metallica or Kate Bush. I was out to him. My trust in him never wavered because he was always a true friend. Dan and I would share many beers together during our time on that boat.

The few friends I had real connections with were invariably in different social groups. I held no loyalty to any group exclusively. I didn't do it consciously but looking back I can see how it was advantageous to have some social connections in several different groups. It made it more likely someone would advocate for me in mixed company. If you keep all gay company, people start to talk.

If someone was even remotely kind to me, I was kind in return. In my naivety, I talked often and frequently with people I knew and felt I could trust. I told them about specific sexual encounters I had. I told them many details about a variety of experiences. There was a very blurry line between the sex positive shame-free queer culture of San Diego, and the rigid military culture that existed within it.

My oversharing wasn't about a lack of morality. I did it in the context of celebrating this part of my actual self. These weren't just things I did. This was a part of my identity, my humanity, and in all my years of being me, I never understood that until I met other gay people, like Vinnie and Lee.

The military might have been rigid and it was far from perfect, but I enjoyed my life. I was happy. Until it happened.

I was standing in morning ranks for uniform inspection. This happened much less frequently than it did in bootcamp and was far less traumatic but still evoked some anxiety. Once the inspection was over my butterfly settled and I turned to walk back to my bunk to change out of my dress uniform. I stopped short of the entrance to the birthing area when I heard a chief petty officer call my name. He said to report topside (upstairs) to meet with military police who were waiting for me at the quarterdeck.

Forget the butterflies. Whatever I felt in my gut now was not a flutter. It was a swarm. I felt sick. The military police didn't just show up and chat with people. Something was wrong. Something was very wrong.

"What do they want.?" I muttered.

"Just go. They are waiting." Said the chief.

I walked to the stairwell. I felt weak and heavy. I was scared. Could this be about the gay thing? Naw, nothing had really happened. I hadn't been stupid enough to do anything on board the ship after all. That's what got people busted.

What if someone in my family died? Would the police notify me? Is that what this was? I tried to think frantically. My friend Dan's brother had died tragically in a drowning accident last year. Did the police notify him? I couldn't remember. Fuck!

I approached the quarterdeck to see two officers waiting.

"We need to escort you to base security. You are being placed under investigation for the suspicion of sodomy."

My heart sank.

I was very familiar with the UCMJ (Uniform Code of Military Justice) and its code relating to homosexuals. I had read it many times and chuckled at the absurdity of it.

Article 125 of the Manual of Court Martial concerns sodomy. The text of the statute says that any service member who engages in an "unnatural form of carnal copulation with another individual belonging to the same sex or the opposite sex, or an animal will be held guilty of sodomy."

Penetration, to whatever extent, is enough to build a case for sodomy. Any service member who is found to have sodomized another person or an animal will be punished as directed by a court martial.

I'd read it a thousand times. What proof did they have? How could they possibly prove anything? Had someone taken pictures of something without my consent!? I mean, technically the way this code is written, a service person could be discharged for anal sex with their wife!

I thought about all the misogynistic stories of stupid drunken sailors and their sexual escapades in other countries, objectifying women and making a mockery of other cultures. I didn't see those guys getting escorted to base security!! My fear quickly turned to rage then back to terror. I wanted to puke. I wanted to run. Oh my god this cannot be happening. My whole body ran hot.

I was led to a back room with two rectangular tables. One had a desk lamp on it like the one you see in movies where they interrogate people.

"Seriously?" I thought. "This has got to be a joke. Oh my god how cliche."

A woman entered the room and asked me to state my name and rank. She informed me that she was conducting an investigation on me after some complaints from "various service members" regarding my homosexual conduct.

Her words were still unbelievable to me. The reality was taking several minutes to get through the shock. I was also momentarily confused because this woman who began the interview was what we in the LGBTQ community call a "bull dyke."

I don't say that to be derogatory in anyway. She was butch and she looked awkward in her dress white skirt. I felt betrayed on a whole deeper level that I was being forced to do this with someone who was probably a closeted member of my own community. Fucking cunt. Or maybe they chose a masculine woman, thinking I'd trust her? I doubt it was that calculated honestly.

I kept thinking to myself, "How is it possible that I could experience such love and acceptance, freedom and revelation and in the same goddamn universe, just across town, and then be treated like this?! How can they do this to people?!"

I was horrified. I thought again about the UCMJ wording.

"Any service member who is found to have sodomized another person or an animal will be punished..."

Is this not the goddamn United States of America?! Do I not have rights? An animal? Seriously? So If I had fucked a dog, would we be having the same conversation?!

I was disgusted. I'd never felt such rage. I instantly wished I was back in Monterey. I didn't want to be here. Please let me not be here. I wished I was back home. I wished I was in school. Anywhere but here.

Breathe. I'm just going to keep breathing.

She continued.

"This is an interview. You are not yet under arrest. You have the right to stop this interview at any time by signing this document."

Her large, strong hand slid a piece of paper to me across the desk until it laid in front of me.

"Are you going to cooperate in answering some questions?" She asked. Her voice was firm and stern.

Instantly I scanned my brain to examine my options.

Don't take too long. Think. What the fuck. Ugh, ok: what I wanted to do was grab that fucking piece of paper and yell "I'm stopping this interview!" And storm out.

No. That's stupid. Don't do that. Be smart. You can do this.

This is just a moment. Moments end. Just keep breathing. That's it. That's what I'll do. Play stupid. Deny it all. Find out what they know.

I heard myself speak in a shaky voice. "Yes ma'am. I will cooperate."

Polite. Be polite.

Her tone was snarky and sarcastic. She was already sneering at me and I hadn't even said anything! She was trying to scare me.

"Have you ever been to a gay bar in Seattle Washington by the name of Neighbors?"

Instantly I knew what this was all about. Three months prior our ship had docked in Seattle. I heard there was a great dance club there called Neighbors. I met a guy there. A hot Latino guy who smelled like sexy sweat and Ralph Lauren cologne. We danced and flirted all night. It was intoxicating! He invited me back to his place where we had sex then I went back to the ship.

Well, after an experience like that, you don't just stay home the next night! So, the following night I went back to the same bar, met someone else. We danced, flirted and made out a little. I remember he was an amazing kisser! Like the night prior, this guy also invited me back to his place.

It was pretty dark and I wasn't paying much attention to the details of my surroundings at first. As we were walking down the sidewalk, I thought the journey looked strikingly familiar. We walked up to his front door and sure enough; it was the SAME damn apartment! I had picked up the roommate of the guy I hooked up with the night before! We laughed about it and ended up having a hot three way. It was great story! Hysterical! I was quite proud of that story. I felt no shame about it. It was a great story! Too funny not to share with my friends.

My hands turned icy cold when I tried to recall just how many people I had told. Who had each of them told? Fuck. This is bad. It could have been virtually anyone.

She was staring at me now, waiting for a response.

I stuttered. "What? Uh... No. Psh... I... I haven't been there. Why?"

I was nervous. She knew I was lying.

She began reciting my own story back to me about the two roommates. She sarcastically explained EVERY detail of the story while rolling her eyes in apparent disgust. Whoever turned me in was someone I trusted. She knew EVERYTHING.

As she talked about the kissing and the cologne I interrupted with objections.

"What?! No! I never did that! That wasn't me."

I thought quickly again about where we were in this interrogation process. What was really happening here? How screwed was I?

I was trying to rapidly psychoanalyze the situation. She was trying to intimidate me clearly. She was using the amount of detail convince me that she knew more than she likely did. She wanted me to know how much she knew.

All she needed was my confession. I could sit here and keep denying this as the story unfolded but what if she was getting ready to pull out some photographs of me leaving the bar with these guys?

I started to panic.

I was trying hard to think.

She wouldn't stop talking! She continued with intimate details of the three-way. She wouldn't stop. She just kept talking over me. The more she talked the louder she got and the more pressured her speech became. She wasn't letting up.

I shouted back at her. "You have the wrong person! That wasn't me!!" I called her bluff.

She glared at me. She didn't expect me to yell at her. Oh my god what the fuck was I thinking? Why did I yell? I was being disrespectful and she out ranked me. Fuck! I was screwed. Ugh.

She threw her pencil down on the table in frustration. Now she was yelling too. "Oh! so what you are telling me is that our informant just made all of this up?!"

I felt my face get red hot and my vision was blurry with tears ready to spill down my face at any moment.

No! I thought. I would NOT let this bitch see me cry! I thought back about the distain I had felt towards my stepmother back in high school when she gave me that self-righteous bullshit of being worried about me. I gathered every bit of disgust I had towards my stepmother and I mentally projected it onto this woman.

I was done. I needed to leave before I started crying. If I started crying I was screwed. My voice was louder now to compensate for my growing hysteria in my voice.

"Look, I don't know what you're talking about, but you have the wrong person! You asked me to answer your questions and I have! I'm stopping this interview now!"

Her tone went from hostile to condescending. "That's fine. You can do that. Just sign here." She pointed to the bottom of the page.

I didn't read shit. I just signed it .

"You're free to go. We'll be in touch." She added.

I was pissed and she knew it. I was shaken. She knew that too. I was hoping my trembling legs would let me walk out of the room. I wasn't sure. I saw my signature begin to appear from under my shaky hand and I walked out.

It happened just like that. Every detail. It was surreal.

I walked out of the office and into the parking lot. The building where I had been interrogated was just across the way from where my ship was docked at the pier. It dawned on me that I had no memory of walking from the pier to the building. I dismissed it.

My thoughts were racing. I could feel my pulse beating in my chest. My mouth was so dry it felt like cotton mouth after a hangover. I knew the feeling well. I didn't know what was going to happen. I had to talk to Vinnie. She was my rock.

In the week that followed. I was painfully aware my peers avoided me, both straight and gay. Have you ever watched a drop of Dawn dishwashing liquid in a pan of greasy water? Yeah, it was like that.

I had two friends who approached me. Vinnie was one of them. She explained that the police had been secretly interviewing all my friends, coworkers and people with whom I was acquainted, trying to match the details of their story to what they knew. I had no idea who would lie for me and who wouldn't. What the hell was I thinking telling people my personal business?

The same lady interviewed Vinnie. In true Vinnie fashion, she threw her head back and let out a roar of laughter. "Oh my god. That's crazy! What the hell? That lady came at me, and I just KNEW she was a dyke! I wanted to say, 'Gurl, STOP!'"

Vinnie had a way of making me laugh even when I didn't want to. She knew I needed that. Vinnie was convinced it was going to be fine. If they had evidence against me they would have arrested me right then. They still could, but it didn't make any sense to wait. Meanwhile, all I could do was wait.

Another friend approached me. He was a straight friend named Larry. I was standing out on the fantail, where the anchor is. I was just outside getting some fresh air. The air quality in that ship was horrendous. Everything was stale and recycled. It had been a few days since the interrogation. Larry walked to where I was standing and stood a few feet away from me. I turned to him to say hi.

"Don't!" He said. "Don't look at me. Just listen, ok?"

We both looked out at the pier as he spoke and I listened.

"You are NOT gay. Got it? No matter what they say to you, you are not gay. Understand?"

He was scaring me.

"I'm not even supposed to be talking to you. None of us are. You're my friend and I didn't want to be a dick. You just have to stop telling people things. They are on to you and they are asking a shit ton of questions."

A single tear rolled down my face.

"Ok" I said.

His eyes met mine for a moment.

He whispered,

"You got this. Just lay low for a while."

Larry walked away and we never spoke of it again. I had never come out to him, and he had never admitted to me he knew I was gay. It was just common knowledge. The ship had two fucking thousand people on it, and it was common knowledge, among all of them that I was gay. I felt a looming sense of regret.

Chapter Seventeen
Shunned

On any typical day, I could walk down a passageway and be greeted by people. A "hey what's up." Or a "Marlow! How's it goin'?" was not uncommon. Since this shit storm began things were different. No one greeted me. No one spoke to me. No one made eye contact. I might get a hushed "Hi." Followed by darting glances to make sure they hadn't been seen talking to me.

Aside from Vinnie, Dan and a few others, people avoided me.

The unspoken culture aboard the ship had always been pretty liberal in terms of everyone knowing there were a percentage of us who were gay. The Dixon had always been a place where no one messed with us and few spoke of it outside their social circle. Something had shifted. It wasn't subtle and it wasn't good.

Vinnie and I both began to hear stories about other queer people being investigated. Some were discharged dishonorably. Some were transferred to less desirable work locations. This was no longer just about me. This was a witch hunt. I had heard about shit like this but had no idea it was real. That explains why my gay shipmates who were still closeted didn't want to be associated with me. It wasn't personal they just didn't want to be associated with me for their own safety. I knew officers and people who had plans on retiring from the Navy who were gay. There were a lot of people who had a lot to lose. Their lives and their careers could be ruined.

Daily, the gravity of the culture shift on board the ship was weighing on me. I couldn't sleep. I was losing weight. Some of the straight guys who I didn't even know, now started to give me dirty looks and mumble things under their breath as I walked by. Some made sure I heard, others did not.

I began to get more menial tasks within my department. I even heard my direct supervisor Chief Valdez, who was a chief Petty officer, call me a "fucking cock sucker" to my face, when I hadn't done something correctly.

Being on a ship wasn't like bootcamp where the norm was verbal abuse and intimidation. On the ship there were policies in place to keep everyone safe from behavior like that. What was happening was so far outside the norm that it put everyone on high alert constantly.

If you consider the word homophobia, by definition, it is literally fear. People who were gay were scared of getting dishonorably discharged and people who were not gay were growing more phobic about how many gay people had been around them the whole time without their knowledge and the more scared they became, the more unsafe it became for people like me. It was a powder keg.

It was chow (dinner) time on the mess deck (cafeteria). At this point I had become accustomed to eating alone and staying to myself. I walked across the floor to discard my tray after I finished eating. A shipmate walked up to me, stood directly in front me so that I couldn't pass. He stood there and stared at me. He was a massive man. Probably 6'3, every bit of 300 lbs with big fat hands. He was standing so close to me I could smell the liquor on his breath.

In a loud booming voice, so that everyone could hear him, he shouts. "Someone told me you're a cock suckin' queer. That true?"

I stood motionless. It was rhetorical. There was no right answer.

He paused a moment, I think for effect and to make sure he had everyone's attention. He leaned in even closer and in a loud husky whisper he says:

"If I ever see you on the street. I'll kill you. I'll fucking kill you. You hear me?"

I stood trembling and nodded.

He took a step as if he were going to walk away from me. He hesitated and stepped back in my direction. He wasn't done. People had now began to gather around us. They were waiting for the fight. It was high school on steroids.

He added: "Ya know, when we are out to sea, at night, it gets real dark out there. If you happened to fall overboard, nobody would find you."

The most terrifying part was that he was right. It would take them hours to realize I was gone. The ship's lookouts, at night at least, often didn't really do their jobs. I knew because sometimes I was one of them.

Everyone chuckled and he walked away, satisfied with the audience he had gathered. In that moment he had just given every single person in that room permission to treat me the same way.

That was it. I was done being bullied. I went directly to the Master-at-Arms (kind of like security on the ship and in some case like the police) and said: "I'd like to file a report against Petty Officer Minks for the following violations of the UCMJ:

1.Defamation of character and

2. Communicating a threat.

I'd had all I could take. If they could use their fucked up rules and polices against me, then I had the right to use those same rules and policies to my advantage.

I had a room full of witnesses and there was no denying it happened.

The following week Petty Officer Minks was scheduled to attend a captain's mast (trial) to address the violations. I was required to attend as the victim of said violations. It was like a formal court setting.

The captain read the violations and asked Minks, "Do you have anything to say for yourself?"

This could go a number of ways, I thought to myself.

Minks responded enthusiastically, "Yes! I said those things sir, but you don't understand. Petty Officer Marlow really is a homosexual, sir!"

Oh my fucking god. No he didn't.

The captain didn't skip a beat. He said, "We are here to discuss your behavior, NOT his sexual orientation."

I got lucky. He was the captain of the ship. He could have done anything he wanted in that situation and neither myself nor Minks would have any recourse whatsoever.

Minks was fined hundreds of dollars, demoted in rank and sentenced to what is the equivalent of community service on the ship with no privilege of wearing civilian clothes for 30 days. That last part sounds silly now after all these years, but when you are forced to wear that damn monkey suit, and do extra work, wearing civilian clothes is a big fucking deal. Being found guilty in a court martial and subsequently confined to the ship also involved a significant amount of public shame. Everyone on restriction, as they called it, had a polaroid of their face posted on bulletin boards throughout the ship, indicating they were not allowed to leave.

After that, Minks never spoke another word to me. Not one. He still gave me dirty looks in the passageways but he never threatened me again. He would still take a subtle lunge in his step as he walked past me only to laugh and me when I flinched every time.

Six months after I had originally been called in for that interrogation, I was notified that the investigation against me would be terminated due to "lack of evidence." I struggle, even today, to express with words the depth of release my soul felt when that situation ended. Something shifted in me after that.

If I had to say the most significant thing that my military experience taught me it would be this: "Always question authority."

Learning the value of advocating for myself had become the most important thing in the world to me. It took a long time for the mood on the ship to shift back to a safer place, but the overt hostility decreased dramatically after that.

Many years later, I sat with my now husband as we watched President Obama lift the ban and allow gay and lesbian service members to serve openly. I bawled uncontrollably with pride. I may not have enjoyed my time in the Navy, but I envied those who were now able to do it openly.

With 2,000 people on the ship there was never a shortage of people to hang out with. Because we repaired and supplied submarines, it also meant that many of us befriended submariners. My friend Dan had been transferred from a sub. Through Dan, I would meet people I might not have otherwise spent a lot of time with. One of those people I will refer to here as "Mike" for reasons of privacy.

I honestly never got to know Mike all that well, just as a friend of Dan and few other common friends. I think it was more accurate to say Mike and I knew of one another. I had a small S-10 pick up truck at the time and having a vehicle often gave you a boost in popularity.

One day mike asked me to take him to a friend's house. He said he was in a hurry and couldn't wait for the bus. I had nothing better to do so I agreed. We arrived at the friend's house and Mike went in. A few minutes later he came back out holding a small brown paper bag. I don't know why I didn't ask what he had in the bag. I just didn't.

Because Mike was known for being somewhat of a partier, it was not anything out of the ordinary that he asked me to stop at Circle K to get a six pack before heading back to his apartment. While he was in the store, I couldn't help but wonder what was so urgent that he couldn't wait for the bus and of course what was in the bag. He had left it casually in the passenger seat. He hadn't tried to hide it so I thought I'd take a peek before he got back.

It was a gun. I quickly wrapped it back up and placed the bag back on the seat.

When he came back to the car I asked, "Dude! What the hell?! A gun? Seriously? What if I get pulled over? I really do not appreciate you not telling me before bringing this in my car!"

I was pissed and had already started to feel pretty used. He apologized, minimized the situation and that was it. We drove back to his apartment where he let himself in and I went home.

That night Mike used that gun to shoot himself in the head while his girlfriend was at work. She came home to find his body. He used me to get that gun.

I know I didn't pull the trigger but sometimes I can't help but wonder if he would have had more time to think to change his mind if I hadn't given him that ride that day. I don't overtly blame myself for his death, but a part of me will always wonder that.

It was years before I told Dan I had unknowingly helped him get the gun.

As I've mentioned, I made friends easily back then. I remember feeling such a sense of comradery within different groups. I think, more quickly than it might have been in a more normal civilian environments. Many of us trauma bonded. I found the longevity of these friendships to be completely unpredictable. They were people with whom I was quite close. Today, I couldn't tell you many of their names and have lost touch with most of them, but Dan, for example, is still a dear friend to this day.

Vinnie and I kept in touch over the years. She kept that sharp quiet wit and only those in her inner circle were privileged enough to experience it. She moved back to Colorado after the navy. the VA awarded her 100% disability from war-time trauma. I think she was taking some art classes there as well which didn't surprise me. She had a nostalgic, artistic creativity. In later years, after the navy she even wore those black rimmed eyeglasses with little granny gemstones in the corners of the frame. She had no fear of sticking out and she did it fabulously!

She was very open about her struggles with cervical cancer. She shared her journey with chemo and how that alone nearly killed her. She became quite the advocate and cancer survivor in her community.

I remember her telling me when she started getting night sweats again, how if it was cancer again, she would not consider chemo as a treatment option, and she didn't. Vinnie's second battle with cancer was one she did much more pain free while she maintained a higher quality of life, till the end. She shared with no one just how sick she was nor the progression of her cancer. She alone held that information. Vinnie died alone in a hospital room. There were no people gawking at her or crying over her. She died with a sense of autonomy and privacy that she cherished. I struggled with that secrecy and personalized it at first, but I'll always hold a secret magical place in my heart for Vinnie Hoffman, may she rest in peace.

Chapter Eighteen
Phoenix

After four years of diversity that I could not have fathomed and trauma I could not have imagined, I had learned a couple things. The first was that I was a survivor. The second was that I was not ready to go back to Ohio. I spent the past four years under a thin veil of secrecy. I served my full term, received an honorable discharge and was able to leave the military with all my benefits intact, a good conduct medal and a dessert store medal, and I earned every bit of it! Now that I was free to be as queer as I wanted to be there was no way I was ready to run back into the closet.

San Diego had provided me with a gay world that the navy kept just beyond my reach. I could move around in queer crowds and clubs on the weekends in the first few years in the navy but after the investigation, I went out much less. I couldn't afford the risk. I counted the days until I didn't have to resort to meeting guys in dangerous situations like parks at night. I was tired of looking over my shoulder.

Vinnie and I now shared an apartment since her break up with Lee. Vinnie was my best friend and confidant. She knew the shit I had been through in the Navy, and it was a massive relief that I could not only finally be myself, but share that with her. Life was great!

I had met a guy a few months before my discharge date and had fallen in love for the first time. I fell hard. He was a beautiful Puerto Rican boy in his 20s. I found his black hair and dark skin exotic and intoxicating. He smelled of designer cologne and his warm smile melted me. His name was Oscar. He lived in New Jersey and was only on vacation in San Diego when we met at a dance club called Rich's. I'd had plenty of random and anonymous sex, but this was different. This was more. It was like hormones mixed with electricity in my stomach. Every touch sent a jolt through my entire being and I was blissfully lost in the magic.

We spent the entire weekend together - every minute. When it was time for him to leave, I went to the airport with him. We held one another and wept. It was crazy. I kept thinking this didn't really happened to real people. I thought these kinds of experiences were only for characters in books and coming of age films, yet there I was; a sobbing mess in the airport with snot running out of my nose.

Oscar and I talked on the phone every day. Back in those days there were no cell phones or text messages. We each had digital pagers, and we would buzz one another all day with secret flirty codes that made each of us smile goofy smiles. We provided each of our friends and coworkers with lovesick eye rolls and knowing grins as our relationship unfolded.

Oscar came to visit me once a month in San Diego. When he wasn't traveling to see me, I was traveling to see him. After about a year, it became clear that the feelings we had for one another weren't going away anytime soon. I was struggling a bit financially. I was finding San Diego pretty expensive. I was working at a pet store and had no formal education so customer service jobs were all I had at my disposal to support myself.

During one of our nightly conversations on the phone, Oscar suggested that we move to Phoenix, Arizona. He explained that he had a brother who lived there who was also gay and said we could live with him and his partner till we got jobs and got on our feet. We longed to be together, and we were spending insane amounts of money traveling back and forth, so I agreed.

The plan was for me to move to Phoenix and Oscar would move down the month after. He flew out from New Jersey and we packed up my car and drove to Phoenix. His brother and his partner were welcoming and supportive.

The next month Oscar had some financial obstacles that prevented him from his move. The month after that he was "unsure about his job." The month after that he "wasn't ready." This went on for two years. He would still come to visit me just as before but the long-awaited move never happened. I had uprooted my life and moved to Phoenix for nothing. I was gutted.

My first time falling in love had turned into my first heartbreak. Much like the romance itself, the absence of it was equally impactful. If I were to describe our love as the most all-encompassing intoxication, I would most certainly have to describe the breakup as the most gut-wrenching hangover my soul could have endured. Because we were both so young and inexperienced we took our hurt out on one another and the ending of our relationship was not pretty. It was ugly and messy. I felt abandoned like a puppy who had been kicked in the ribs and left on the side of the road after having been promised a home.

In retrospect I was pathetic. I learned much from my relationship with Oscar. I learned what it felt like to be loved, to be wanted. And I learned how dangerous it can be to give myself so deeply and so unconditionally. I was painfully codependent. That would be the beginning of a long road of self-discovery in how I navigated relationships - what I would put up with and what I wouldn't.

Oscar and I did find one another on Facebook a few years ago. Over 30 years had passed since I was that young insecure socially awkward twink. We are now good friends - older, wiser versions of ourselves. He still has the same job in New Jersey and has a partner. We chat occasionally. It's nice to revisit that sweet spot in my mind when we talk. I observe it from a distance fondly.

While I was waiting for Oscar, I hadn't put my entire life on hold. After all, I still needed friends and a social life. I stayed in Phoenix for 5 years after that. I worked in a pet store in Paradise Valley Mall where I met some wonderful friends with whom I maintain relationships to this day.

I must say, one of the most alluring friendships was not someone I saw often, but rather the niece of a friend. Her name was Jessica. She was my first exposure to paganism and lived a few doors down from me in the same apartment complex. Jessica was a beautiful young biracial woman with long kinky hair, light brown skin and lots of cool jewelry.

She had an undying loyalty to the band The Grateful Dead though honestly, she was rocking some serious Stevie Nicks energy. Although she was actually a few years younger than me, she had a maternal instinct so warm and loving that she made me feel safe. I remember her apartment smelling of essential oils and being adorned with tapestries with a hint of African roots – the kind you'd find in a headshop. I deeply admired her raw honesty about her struggles with addiction, as well as her love of all things related to Siberian Huskies. A loving smirk still graces my face when I think about the stunning features of the breed as well as their fierce independence; that was the essence of Jessica.

To this day, she is a friend who I could call at 3am to hide a body and she'd say, "Ok well I'm sure you had a good reason. Let's talk about it." Total witchy vibe. I love her to death.

I had many different jobs while I lived in the desert. I worked as a pool boy for a few summers, traveling around the city cleaning rich people's in-ground pools. It sounds like a porno waiting to happen right? Sorry to disappoint. Nothing ever happened. All the right situations were there,

I was just far too awkward to ever initiate anything.

I know what you're thinking. The irony is not lost on me. When I was in the Navy, I actively engaged in risky sexual behavior. It was titillating and exciting. Now, in the desert, the excitement was more of a moving target.

I also worked in a call center for Bank One where I provided Spanish speaking customer service. I hated that job but it was my first professional Spanish speaking opportunity. That was a big accomplishment for me. Living in San Diego and Phoenix it was not hard to practice Spanish, but this was the first time I used it for employment.

I think back to that time with pride. Yes, I was heartbroken, but I picked myself up and tried to make some money and clean up some credit issues. I was learning what it meant to me an independent gay man and I liked it.

Phoenix is a sprawling metropolis in the desert. Even then, it had a modest size LGBT community and there were a couple gay bars within relative proximity. I loved it but had no real personal attachment to it either, after all I was only there because Oscar had asked me to come. Since that relationship had ended, and so bitterly, I was finding less and less reason to stay yet had no real direction.

My roommate, Chris, had also been my coworker at the Pet Pad in the mall. She and I had become good friends and had lived together for a few years at this point. She and her husband had decided to pack up what little they had and move to San Francisco. They invited me to come and although I said "sure!" I was incredibly intimidated.

San Francisco was a real city! I had, unbeknownst to me, become quite content with having some elbow room and being able to navigate Phoenix. And although it wasn't my dream place to live it had become familiar, comfortable. When I was there with a broken heart, it was my new friends who had invited me to smoke a bong, climb Camelback

Mountain, or go tubing on the river. I hadn't realized it but I had grown a few roots and transplanting myself would not be a painless process.

I'd like to stick a pin in this part of the story for a moment and point out some pivotal things that I have come to understand looking back on this part of my life.

While I technically had been out to my family, it still wasn't something any of us ever really talked about. My queerness had become this thing that everyone knew, but I didn't have any desire or courage to actually address on any level. I was totally content with the way things felt.

In terms of my being gay, the fact of the matter was: I was able to have sex with pretty much whomever I wanted. People in Phoenix were pretty normal, and navigating new cultures in the Mexican and Native American friends I'd met didn't take much adjustment for me.

Jessica had also spent some time in the Bay Area and spoke of it fondly. This low-level stress gave me a bit of confidence and excitement for what San Francisco could mean for me. I was 29, attractive and had the libido of a 17-year-old. I was good to go! I had no idea what I was walking towards.

I said my goodbyes to the gay Denny's on Camelback Road and Zorbas, the adult bookstore in Scottsdale, and put the saguaros in my rearview mirror and headed west. All I knew was that I saw a light at the end of the tunnel and I was pretty sure it was a trolley car.

Chapter Nineteen
San Francisco

Chris and I lived in a drafty old Victorian house in Alameda just across the bay from the city. It was much cheaper than living in the city so it was a great place to start. Alameda was a bit like Mayberry from the Andy Griffith show. It was quiet and unassuming. Though nestled up against the raw streets of Oakland, it was also not always so innocent. It was pretty uneventful but it was nice. It wasn't too far from the city. A 30-minute BART ride under the bay and bam! You were there.

I don't know what I expected; nothing really. I was like a deer in the headlights. In my first visit to the Castro I encountered the Sisters of Perpetual Indulgence. What in the loving hell?? For those of you who have not have the pleasure of their acquaintance, basically they are a group of drag queens dressed as nuns with white painted faces. Much like Mary Anne Singleton in Tales of the City, I was in shock, overwhelmed yet strangely intrigued. The Sisters of Perpetual Indulgence, also called Order of Perpetual Indulgence is a charity, protest, and street performance organization that uses drag and religious imagery to call attention to sexual intolerance and satirizes issues of gender and morality. It is common to see these drag nuns at fundraisers in the city and often in the bars and gayborhoods. At first encounter they are visually shocking to the naïve visitor. That's the point. They get your attention. They have become a staple in the San Francisco area and in time I found their presence quite endearing and empowering. I mean, it takes balls to do that kind of activism!

I was familiar with the gays of San Diego. They were fabulous, sometimes flamboyant and fun, but I always had the experience of "putting it away," so to speak, and going back to my ship. Then in phoenix, the most flamboyant thing I'd seen was queer cowboys at a gay country western bar called Charlie's where I learned to line dance. But this?! This was an entirely different universe all together. I was lost and I loved it!

I had always found myself existing in environments where the expectation was to fit in or at the very least acclimate. San Francisco is an experience that is forever changing and evolving. It's the treasure hunt for precious moments and experiences. I would later discover the most painful and pivotal moments in queer history that took place in this city and how humbled I was to witness and walk in the footsteps of queer people before me; people whose pain and raw courage made it possible for me to be as unassuming as I needed to be and for someone else to be as "in your face" as they needed to be. It was an environment that was all encompassing. Any kind of person fit no matter where they came from or where they were going.

I think of all the people I met in my decade in the city, I may have met five who were San Francisco natives. I had never conceived of this place on the planet. We were all plants in a strange little terrarium where none of us originated. I even crossed paths with two friends from High school who lived in the city the same time I did. Greg and Mark were high school sweethearts.

They were closeted, to me anyway. They have now been together for 30 years! That still amazes me. They are both dear friends now. We had different circles of friends both then and now, but it was so nice to talk to them as other queer people and be able to connect and relate in that genuine way. It's refreshing. Ironically, I always felt a bit out of their circle in high school. At the time I assumed it was because they really didn't like me. The reality, however, was that they were both struggling, especially Greg I think, with their own sexual orientation, as was I.

My career was one of the many gifts I took with me when I moved from that city. Although I had a couple of dead-end jobs at the start, I found a passion for mental health, in particular, psychotherapy. I found pieces of myself that I didn't know existed in that city. Pieces of trauma from an abusive childhood, fragments of my past, all formed together to create a set of core values that gave me permission to redefine.

I lived in San Francisco for ten years. For nine and a half of those years, I spent with Mario. When I met him, he was working at a non-profit sheltering people with HIV, guiding them through their darkest days. I remember watching him patiently navigate complex cases, offering not just a bed but a lifeline to those the world too often forgot. In the Bay Area's tangled web of social services, his compassion stood out like a beacon; it was my very first glimpse into the soul of mental health work. Thanks to Mario's social connections, I met the warm-hearted mentors who would show me the ropes of psychology—and, more importantly, inspire me to believe that one person's empathy can change a life.

One of the places that helped me discover parts of myself was the New College of California in the Mission District. It's no longer there today, but this tiny little bohemian school offered BA completion programs in various subjects and a subsequent master's program in earthy type careers. I had taken classes at local community colleges in Phoenix and off and on in San Francisco, but I always got frustrated and dropped out. I never thought I was smart enough to go to college and was told as much growing up. It's still chilling to me how the human psyche holds on to those dysfunctional echoes from our past and allows our brain to reclaim them as truths.

I was thrilled to learn that, despite jumping from school to school, along the way I had managed to collect enough credits to qualify for the BA completion program offered at New College. It was a 12-month program offered in a cohort setting. Like many of the buildings along common streets in the city, New College looked like nothing more than a doorway off the street, a modest lobby closed off with an black iron gate. The lobby was cluttered with old house plants someone had been growing for years and a couple of water features to top off the Zen energy created by the sounds of the trickling water.

You almost didn't even notice the sounds of the MUNI buses up and down the street once you were inside. It was a place of learning, not one of pretentious scholars from an Ivy League school, but of life teachings and history. I can still smell the hallways, the old stairwells that held untold stories of generations past.

There were also some significant people who helped me discover some of my own hidden talents. The most influential of these was my undergraduate advisor, Harry Britt. I'd never heard his name. I had no idea who he was. As far as I was concerned, he was just some middle-aged college professor who was teaching a course here and there. He showed up in jeans and a casual button-down shirt and was soft spoken. He was a larger, husky man with grey hair and a soft, round face. He was sweet and approachable.

Many instructors who lasted at New College encouraged group discussions as a core teaching method. Sometimes these discussions were facilitated by some text, a guest speaker or other means. Harry was one of these professors who allowed us not just to speak our minds but to really speak to one another, to debate, to learn from one another. Harry sometimes lost track of time in his lectures about the years he'd spent in the gay rights movement. I never really questioned how much of this history he had experienced himself or if it was second-hand

114

knowledge. I just assumed he was a good storyteller. Some people just have that ability - that talent of drawing you in and holding your focus on every word, making you wonder how the sentence was going to end. Harry was like that.

One day in particular, he was telling us about what the city was like during the Stonewall riots in the 60s. If you are queer or any member of the LGBT community, you know how important that time in history was for our community. Then, without a hint of ostentatiousness or hesitation for emphasis, he begins to tell us how he was best friends with Harvey Milk!

Wait. What?!

I'm not sure my classmates knew this either, because you could see the admiration and awe seep into their expressions and their smiles. For me, not having grown up in this area of the country and certainly not having had any connection or exposure to queer culture, it was such an honor to be able to talk to a man who knew Harvey well.

I remember asking Harry if we could just skip our break halfway through class so we could finish listening to his story, which he was sharing with us. As tears filled his eyes, he shared his memories of the week before Harvey was murdered. Harvey had called Harry and told him that he was certain someone was going to try to assassinate him and that if that person were to succeed, he wanted Harry to continue his political work towards equality and gay activism. As far as I know, Harvey did not disclose to Harry whether he knew who the assassin would be.

The following week, November 27th, 1978, supervisor Harvey Milk was shot to death along with San Francisco Mayor George Moscone at City Hall by former supervisor Dan White. White was convicted of voluntary manslaughter and not first-degree murder. His defense was that he allegedly suffered from temporary low blood sugar, leaving him with a diminished mental capacity. This is antecedently referred to as the Twinkie defense. The state of California would later abolish the diminished capacity criminal defense largely due to what is now referred to in history as the "White Night Riots."

It was the most violent backlash the LGBT community unleashed since the Stonewall riots. Dan White came from a family of privilege. His crime brought a great deal of shame to his family. One year after his short prison stay, Dan White completed suicide. While I do not find myself in complete alignment with the celebration that took place in the streets upon the news of his death, there is a part of me that understands it.

Harry shared those personal stories with us that day among others about what it felt to get that call from Dianne Feinstein that the riots had began, the fear, the rage, all of it. He shared it with us; those eight other people in that room and I will forever be grateful for it and my relationship with Harry.

In my humanity and in my heart, I will always carry such honor, pain, and unrelinquishing respect for the people who lost their lives that day, for the people who loved them, and for the rights, visibility, and evolution those tragic events brought our community.

Chapter Twenty
Building a Life

By this time, I was 29 years old. I looked around at my life and discovered that I had grown up. Finishing my undergrad was something I never thought was possible. All those years of believing I couldn't succeed! What a horrible, self-deprecating waste of time to subscribe to that notion.

Mom and Dad both flew out to California for my graduation, which surprised me. It was the first time they had spent any time together in over 20 years. I'm certain my mom's husband didn't know Dad was there. It was completely platonic, but her husband's ego and low self-esteem could not have handled that.

I remember Mom and Dad buying me a card for my graduation. They signed it, "Love Mom and Dad." I cried. I still have that card. They were proud of me, finally.

Immediately following the success of my bachelor's degree, I applied to, and was accepted into, the MFT program (master's in marriage and family therapy) at New College of California. I had gotten quite a foothold in the mental health community, but I would never advance without a higher degree. Harry Britt provided me with a glowing letter of recommendation, and I began my coursework later that fall.

While in school, I also worked at halfway houses as a fill-in counselor for several different organizations and quickly became aware of my skills in helping people.

The coursework was challenging but not impossible. I kept waiting for it to feel insurmountable; It never did. I excelled in academia and finished my first year of grad school with a 3.8 GPA.

Another turn of events that I would never have dreamt of was that my being gay had seemingly become a non-issue to my parents. I was grown now, living in California. I was a responsible college graduate with a professional job. How I lived my life in the midst of that, really was none of their business, and they knew it. Furthermore, I only visited Ohio maybe once a year. I would come in for a Christmas or other occasion, stay for a week, then head back to California, where I had built a life. I existed there.

My family knew I lived with Mario; they knew the nature of our relationship. I wasn't sure if time had softened their views or if the distance helped with their tolerance, but that tolerance started looking more and more like acceptance as the years progressed. Even so, I still cringed at using the word "gay" in their presence.

Mario would sometimes join me on my trips back to Ohio for the holidays. My sister even insisted that he come to her wedding. It had been a few years into the relationship at that point, and nothing was changing anytime soon. I think my parents saw that if they wanted to be a part of my life, this was also a part of that experience of having me for a son.

Just to shed some insight into how much had shifted, at my sister's wedding, Mario and I were sitting at our table, and my mom's husband walked over to us. I felt my stomach sink to my knees. God, please, please don't make a scene.

He reached out to shake Mario's' hand and introduced himself and said, "Nice to meet you."

That was it! This was the same man who threatened me in the fifth grade about bringing home a "queer" and I had done just that! Ha! I remained in disbelief, but what a relief it all was!!

San Francisco, as well as Mario's social circle, taught me a lot about who I was and who I wanted to be. His family and friends, all almost exclusively Latino, reminded me of Bolivia and the life I found there. I think that fondness contributed to putting up with and tolerating much in that relationship that I probably shouldn't have.

The sometimes in-your-face kind of queer culture in San Francisco taught me many things. Among those was the fact that I still had a significant amount of internalized homophobia. I only call it that in retrospection. At the time, it presented itself as judgment.

My family, my hateful, abusive family, had accepted me! And I had to move heaven and earth to make that happen! (I actually did nothing. Looking back, I have no idea why I gave myself credit for that, but for some reason at the time, this is how I needed to understand it.) If something simple, like not using the word gay in their company, was something I had to do for me to bring Mario home with me, then so be it. The sacrifice was worth it to me.

In my relationship with Mario, I found potential for a future. I found hope. I made many reparations to keep hope alive, but at the time, I was willing to do that.

Our relationship had become quite domestic - in many ways, not all that different from many straight couples we knew. One of the many things I love about the city is the diversity in the queer community. I haven't always felt that way, and at the time, I did not understand why. Now, I think I do.

Internalized homophobia is an experience many queer people have for a myriad of reasons. Some of which may be societal or cultural. It's those messages that we get in our everyday life that tell us we are not enough. It could be from something as passive as not seeing ourselves represented in mainstream culture, movies, commercials, etc. It could also be direct messages from our families of origin, where our queerness is not celebrated, not even acknowledged, and in some cases, even punished.

Furthermore, these messages of self-hatred and self-fear also result in hateful legislation and a lack of protective laws for our community. Before marriage equality, for example, I felt a sting of unworthiness every time I witnessed a heterosexual couple become legally married, when I was not granted the same right. My point is, internalized homophobia comes at us from a million different directions, and it's not just one origin.

I noticed gay pride was a big trigger for me. I wanted a family. I wanted to be a father. Because the law, at that time, did not support these dreams, it was like we needed permission or had to convince the government and lawmakers that we were normal.

While many people saw pride as a time to be as flamboyant and vulgar as they wanted, to me, this was not pride. In fact, I was threatened by it. The front page of any given newspaper or the top story on the 11 o'clock news the day after Pride is never the average-looking gay couple. It is usually something more for shock value, like a bearded drag queen in lace panties prancing down the street. I felt threatened by this. Why? Because I felt that image would make it harder for people to see us as normal. It would make us less likely to be taken seriously. I was still operating in a heteronormative mindset thinking I needed the permission of straight people, in order to exist.

There are many places in the world, luckily, where that drag queen has every right to prance down the street and celebrate his/her expression of his/her queerness as the gay male couple or lesbian couple pulling the red wagon with the toddler. One shouldn't need the permission from the other to exist. I embrace that and understand that now. Then, I felt threatened by the trans person or person in drag who didn't necessarily pass because of my own internalized homophobia. I had fought so hard in the Navy simply not to be exposed that, internally, I was still afraid.

I had many heteronormative ideas about my relationship with Mario. One major growing concern was that I was reminded of a dream: I always wanted to be a dad. Growing up, realizing my queerness provided a complication I chose to ignore. Because my sense, or rather, my hope of being gay, was something that I could just one day stop being, the following assumption was that when that day came, I could more seriously look at becoming a father. As I matured and understood being gay for who I was and not for an activity I was doing, the dream of becoming a father became further and further from my reality.

Something that awakened this dream was seeing my sister give birth to her first child. In addition, my peers from high school were all having children. My cousins, some much younger than me, were all starting families. Having a child was a rite of passage in my family and often in our culture. The fact that I didn't see that on my timeline bothered me more and more.

I had many conversations with Mario over the years about my growing need to be a dad. We researched adoption, surrogacy, and explored many options. However, Mario accepted all of them in the context of "Sure, one day we can do that." Furthermore, I was always the one to bring it up. He never did. This fact was not lost on me and was a great cause of increasing anxiety. I found Mario's lack of enthusiasm and lukewarm agreement infuriating. Most of my life, I had been exceedingly far from seeing myself as a father, and now with this relationship and domestic life we had settled into, I was closer than ever. It hadn't been an intentional journey, but it was where I found myself. The question I had was: "Why not?"

Mario was a Mexican-American. His parents had come from Mexico to California before he was born. His father was extraordinarily artistic and quickly established himself as a master jeweler. He made, and still makes, a great deal of money. Mario's father was well known for his custom designs - he designed a belt buckle for Elvis Presley in the 70's. Compensating for their humble beginnings and their desire to follow a dream in the States, Mario's parents had raised their children with the finest of everything. Live-in servants, extravagant and spontaneous vacations, designer clothing - this was how Mario grew up.

Unfortunately, with these fine things, Mario had also been fostered with the notion that he was "just a little bit" better than most people. Cleaning a toilet or getting his hands dirty were simply things he saw as beneath him. The first few years of our relationship I had mistaken his arrogance and entitlement as a cocky kind of endearment. In retrospect, this was a huge red flag because I was very attracted to that quality. I found it attractive. He never really needed me. Years later, that sense of attractiveness had devolved into something very different. His arrogance became an increasingly problemmatic issue in our relationship that I found tedious to navigate.

Mario and I were together for 9 ½ years. It was not all good or bad. We simply reached a point where we were no longer good for one another. The symptoms of this fact presented themself in various kinds of dysfunction. I cannot, however, say that he was categorically an evil person. He wasn't. Mario was actually one of the first people who made me feel I could go to college, that I was smart. He's also one of the first people to manipulate me to the point that I questioned my own sanity. He was a master at that.

Chapter Twenty-One
The Goodbye

I sat in the apartment we had shared for almost a decade, surrounded by the familiar remnants of our life together—photographs of vacations, mismatched coffee mugs, and the art on the walls. Each object felt like a betrayal now, conspiring to remind me of what I was losing. Ten years of love, laughter, and quiet Sunday mornings unraveled into a single decision - one that ripped through me like a jagged edge. I loved him. God, I loved him.

We wanted different lives. Paths that diverged so sharply we couldn't pretend to walk together anymore. I wanted a family, a child to pass down stories and traditions to, while he wanted money and looked down his nose at my dreams.

And so, after years of the same circular arguments, the same rehearsed apologies and half-hearted compromises, I stood on the front porch of that Victorian house we shared and I cried. I cried so hard, knowing that to stay was to let my dreams rot.

There was silence, but not the peaceful kind. It was heavy, laced with echoes of our fights, the warmth of our laughter, and the nights on the balcony smoking a joint when we thought our love could conquer anything.

I had replayed our last conversation endlessly in my mind, searching for cracks in his logic, for some sign that I could turn back. But the truth, no matter how much it hurt, was clear: this relationship, once my entire life, was now over.

It hurt to think about those moments, to know they would never come again. It wasn't fair.

So I cried. I let the sobs tear through me like a storm. I wasn't ready for the light yet; the darkness was still too raw, too all-encompassing. But somewhere in the back of my mind, I knew that one day, the pain would dull, the memories would soften, and I would learn to love myself enough to move forward. For now, though, all I could do was sit in the wreckage of what once was and wait for the pieces to stop cutting so deeply.

Driving that U-Haul truck east across the Ohio state line was a significant moment. I didn't know what was going to happen. I didn't even know what I wanted to happen. My only driving force was that I wanted to adopt a child and now that my family accepted me for who I am, all things were possible. I wanted to offer my child a multi-generational experience. I wanted to give him/her opportunities of overnights and grandma's house, birthday parties with cousins, and camping trips with aunts and uncles.

Despite being heartbroken and emotionally lost, the drive to create a family propelled me forward. There was no time to wallow in self-pity. Part of my resolve was based on the fact that I knew I was choosing to be a single parent. I knew I couldn't do it alone. I needed my family's support, but what I didn't need was a man to complete me.

Moving back to Ohio wasn't a decision I made lightly. I was halfway through my master's in marriage and family therapy. Part of me wished I could stick it out another year and finish school before I moved back home, but I was far too heartbroken. The old familiar places would have been too painful, so I left.

After years of living in California—a place where I had found parts of myself I didn't even know existed. I had found acceptance and the courage to embrace who I was fully. Unfortunately, San Francisco was simply too expensive. After having transplanted myself more than a decade prior, I felt the weight of returning to the roots I had worked so hard to escape. Ohio wasn't just a state to me; it was a memory, a mirror reflecting the fractured relationships, whispered disapproval, and cold stares I had grown up with. It wasn't just moving home; it was walking willingly into a storm I knew might never settle.

I told myself it was for the child I hoped to adopt one day. A dream I held close, fragile and full of promise. I wanted this child to know the love of a family, even if that family had never truly accepted me. I imagined holiday dinners and birthdays filled with laughter, a child running through the yard, cousins to play with, and grandparents to dote on them. It was a vision I clung to, even as I braced for the sacrifices it would demand of me.

My parents had always been polite about my life in California. They even took turns visiting from time to time. Politeness, I discovered was a thin veil for what is left unsaid. i could see it in the way my mother's lips tightened in disapproval when I mentioned a partner or how my father changed the subject when conversations drifted too close to anything personal.

Their love was conditional, wrapped tightly in their own expectations and narrow views. Returning home felt like swallowing shards of glass, a quiet kind of pain that cut deep but never spilled blood.

The first few weeks were a blur of driving through old neighborhoods and reconnecting old relationships. I was trying to see what I could piece back together.

Family gatherings were the hardest. Sitting in a parent's living room, surrounded by people who saw me as a shadow of what they wanted me to be, I felt like an imposter in my own skin.

Here, I felt like a ghost, a reflection of who I was, haunting the places I once knew.There were moments of light, small glimmers of hope that reminded me I might fit in somewhere. A niece or a nephew who asked innocent questions about my life out of curiosity, then got a glance of instant disapproval from their parents if they got too excited about anything I had to say.

The microaggressions were saturated in homophobia. They came in waves. It was unpredictable. There were times I could genuinely connect with different people in my family but more and more that connection would come at an increasing price of constantly editing myself.

The changing seasons offered a bittersweet comfort, the crisp autumn air reminded me of simpler times, before I fully understood the complexities of who I was and what that meant in a place like this.

Moving back to Ohio wasn't easy. It was a journey of sacrifice, resilience, and hope. I assumed the road ahead would be difficult, littered with misunderstandings and moments of heartbreak. I saw the same old dysfunction I knew as a kid. It was still all there but it was different. Some of it had softened in time.

The overt homophobic slurs of my youth had now morphed into casual looks of disapproval and invitations to church to save my soul. That's better, right?

I boldly tried to carve out a place for myself in a community no longer meant for me.

Despite this, I hoped that my effort to build bridges would speak to my character, that somehow they would see my efforts and find meaning in that.

Still sitting in my father's garage, after 36 years, there it was: my brother's old headstone. Ugh, Jesus Christ! Seriously? I asked my dad if I could have it. He agreed. I just purchased my first home. I built a pond in my backyard. Next to the pond, I placed Timothy's headstone surrounded by wildflowers. This is the place where I go to think. I think about what kind of person he may have been. I think about my responsibility to live a life when he was not provided the luxury to do so.

When the Bedbugs Bite

Chapter Twenty-Two
Children's Services

M any changes took place with my family in Ohio during my years in California. I visited my family once or a twice a year and became somewhat aware of them. Babies were born, people got married, people died and life evolved, taking with it all passengers like a train through time. No one was exempt.

Despite my awareness of many changing dynamics in my family there remained unexplored interpersonal complexities I simply couldn't understand without living there. One of those things was my relationship with my sister.

Although she and I remained extraordinarily close as we became adults, she had a different social circle than I did. We were both aware of it. Still, I always stayed with her and her husband when I visited Ohio and she came to San Francisco once to stay with Mario and I.

I had spend much of my adult life traveling. I experienced many different cultures and norms. My time in San Francisco, alone provided many opportunities for recreational drug use and experimentation. I've never been dishonest about that, nor do I feel shame about it. Cannabis use was prevalent in my social circles and often in my home. I had several friends who used it both medicinally and recreationally. I've never had an issue with either. Although I had spent brief moments in my 20s and early 30s experimenting with other substances occasionally, I had always drawn a hard line at needles and any hallucinogen that altered my reality to the extent I lacked control.

Part of my wanting to be a dad was so I could explore those parts of my youth without exposing a child to the instability and unpredictability that many kinds of substance use often cause. This doesn't make me a better person. I simply made different choices.

I won't make excuses for her nor pretend to understand her reasons, but the fact was that my sister had developed a significant habit of taking pills. Pain pills, opioids, muscle relaxers, they were all on the menu. Having a far left liberal outlook on many things in my life, the severity of my sister's habit was something that took time for me to understand fully. She nodded off at family functions, was often visibly impaired at social events, and had fewer and fewer boundaries of when she chose to be high.

As I mentioned before, I had no issue with smoking pot to unwind or even numb, but the pill use and the culture of that use were not something with which I had a lot of experience.

One of the changes my family had undergone due to my sister's use was years of involvement with children's services regarding my sister's two daughters. I watched from a distance and up close, the severity of dysfunction and the lack of ability to actually protect children by the child welfare system. I also watched as my parents and extended family had become forceful enablers in my sister's addiction.

One of the many stunning moments of my parents' enabling behavior was when my youngest niece was born and tested positive for substances, among them being THC. The hospital fulfilled its legal obligation and contacted children's services to report the results.

Although my niece was not removed then, my sister had to agree to a safety plan and deal with a significant amount of bureaucracy to keep her child. It was chaotic and emotional. The doctor who had made the report to children's services had been the family doctor for years. My mother felt betrayed by the doctor, and my entire family rallied against her and refused to continue seeing her. It was the doctor whom my family demonized. That doctor had an ethical and legal obligation. Once again, my sister was the victim of something she created. It was before the legalization of cannabis, and while I certainly did not place any moral judgment on smoking pot, I was still dumbfounded at my sister's unyielding denial that she had to know they would find out once the baby was born.

My father consistently looked down his nose at her and her husband for their use. He made feverish attempts to keep her and her family engaged with the church to compensate for her life choices. My sister was active in the church community and sometimes showed up high at church functions. The muscle relaxers and Xanax would fuel her wobbly entrances into the church parking lot, nodding out during a sermon, while others whispered or pretended not to notice.

My mother's attempts to help my sister often involved funneling money to pay for rent, food, and shut-off notices for utilities. The financial need was endless, resulting in several consecutive years of evictions from various apartments and houses. My parents were there each time to help her transition to the next failed situation.

My sister, with her girls in tow, lived her life in a constant state of self-induced crisis. My oldest niece, then a teenager, shared many stories with me about her life of abuse and neglect. I also carried the weight of having personally witnessed domestic violence situations between my sister and her husband while they were both high. Often, the children were crying in their rooms, listening to the fighting.

Many tearful conversations took place between my parents and myself.

For years, my parents had said things like, "Someone's got to do something" or" Someone has to help those poor girls." It was much like the sentiment of sending thoughts and prayers after a school shooting without outlawing guns.

Although my parents' inclination was typically to meet an immediate financial need my sister had, or to rescue the girls after a tearful phone call due to their parents fighting again, my parents always defaulted back to the notion that my sister knew best and would allow the abuse and neglect to continue. Watching my oldest niece grow was like having a small piece of my sister back.

I had become very close to my niece over the years. As my relationship with my sister deteriorated, my connection with my niece strengthened. Unfortunately, within the context of my family unit, I felt powerless to help her, despite her frequent attempts to reach out to me. It was heartbreaking. It wasn't that no one cared. My sister had set a carefully constructed trap over the years. Anyone who tried to help in a way my sister didn't approve of was cut off from seeing the girls. The children were leverage in a game my sister always won. I had heard the expression in my professional circles, "You'll never win an argument with a drug addict." I was living it. It was the raw truth.

Although I do not recall the specific event that forced my hand, the day came when I felt forced to make a decision. Since my return to Ohio, I had learned that, over the years, many calls had been made to children's services to report my sister. Some calls came from my mom, my dad, and some from people in the community, like the girls' school.

My sister had found the loophole in the system: With only allegations of abuse/neglect and the ability to provide a prescription for the drugs in question, all she had to do was refuse to cooperate. The child welfare system was powerless without a court order or my sister's consent for agency involvement. The nature of the way child welfare laws are written provided my sister with this escape for years.

Even paramedics, who were frequently called to her house when she became unresponsive, would ask to speak to the children alone. As long as Tina was able to mumble an objection in her obviously inebriated state, they couldn't do anything. They had to just leave.

I hired an attorney and filed for custody of both my nieces. My mother and father had relied on my professional knowledge of social service agencies. They often sought my advice. Time and time again, I told them how to file for custody and what to say. Neither of them would do it because everyone was afraid of my sister. She had them all manipulated and bullied into submission.

The evidence and testimony in court were not difficult to prove. A myriad of stories and explanations including but not limited to: my niece jumping from a moving car because my sister was driving impaired, my sister having recently been on life support due to an overdose while the children were in her care, and multiple occasions of both nieces traumatized and calling other family members in crisis because they had not been able to wake their mother. The stories spanned several years and increased in severity down the timeline.

Chapter Twenty-Three
The Beginning of the End

I was awarded temporary custody of both girls. In Ohio, this level of custody can last for a period of up to two years and sometimes beyond. Despite the mounting evidence, it was actually ridiculously difficult to get children's services involved. Caseworkers and their supervisors gave me reasons like "We don't get involved in personal family affairs. "Not only was I fighting my sister, whom I once considered my best friend, but now the very system designed to protect children was refusing to help.

Having worked for children's services I knew damn well that if the agency had formally removed the children themselves, the agencies involvement would have been mandatory, and they would have court orders leaving my sister powerless to resist. Because she had learned over the years to deny the agency access to the girls when they showed up at her front door on numerous occasions to investigate, the agency had no authority.

The child welfare agency reluctantly opened a case to reunite the children with my sister. This goal was contingent on case plan objectives that she and her husband both engage in and successfully complete a certified drug program and domestic violence counseling.

Weekly visits were established so my sister could see her children.

I was actually fine with the goal of reunification because it finally meant my sister would be forced to get help if she wanted her kids back. No more manipulating or using the girls as pawns. She would finally have to face her life choices and hopefully learn to make better ones. This would have been a logical conclusion if it weren't for the fact that my sister was allowed to choose my parents to supervise her weekly visits with the girls. They, of course, looked the other way and broke every rule they could during visits, which, of course, made me look like a raving lunatic if I tried to file contempt over every violation.

They demanded extra time on visits, extra days, and there was always some kind of excuse why they needed more time on each visit. Extended family, who hadn't seen the girls with any kind of consistency, now all had a burning need to see the girls, demanding extensions and more time. If I denied the request, I had to answer in court as to why I was not allowing the girls to see their family. My family had closed ranks. I was a lone person fighting against the entire system, them, and children's services.

Even reports of my youngest niece reporting things that happened during her visits were dismissed as "the child sounded coerced and rehearsed, therefore not credible." It was maddening. I had never seen anything like it. The magistrate actually would roll her eyes during testimony while filing her nails, as if she couldn't be bothered to hear any evidence. She even told us once in court, "I'm not going to allow that because we are trying to reunify."

Over the next two years, I would endure a backlash I could not have predicted in my worst dreams. My sister spent an entire year, not seeking treatment, but trying to assassinate my character both in court and at family gatherings. In line with her pattern of behavior of defense, my parents followed suit.

My Christian father wrote horrible letters and made phone calls to me and my oldest niece, saying she had stolen her sister away from loving family. He once wrote to the courts that I had "snatched the children away from already involved grandparents, intentionally estranging them from family and exposing them to my perverted lifestyle." The truth being, of course, my father often wrote my sister off and discarded her as nothing more than a drug addict who tarnished his Christian image. Her addiction shamed him. My existence shamed him more.

We were bombarded with daily, sometimes hourly, text messages saying I was brainwashing the girls to hate their parents, allegations of my being a heroin addict, a prostitute, and several other absurd attacks that could not have been further from the truth. One of the most maddening elements was the fact that while these allegations were clearly a distraction from the real problem, I had to defend each and every one of them in a court of law.

My mother even brought two of her sisters to court, not as witnesses of any kind, but to be there to hang out in the hallway outside the courtroom to harass me and taunt me verbally. Grown adults behaving like junior high bullies.

The courts allowed this three-ring circus to grow until it imploded. Legal proceedings that should have been handled with some amount of decorum were often nothing more than an episode of the Jerry Springer show.

I was blindsided. The acceptance I thought I had was clearly nothing more than tolerance. If I am being completely honest, I do not believe my parents were consciously aware of the origin of their discomfort. I think the idea of having a gay son who lived 2000 miles away was something they found a way to tolerate, to justify, because I was successful by all other standards. By this time, I had two college degrees, a successful career working as a psychotherapist, I was a wartime veteran in the armed services, and STILL I was not enough. When I returned to Ohio, I was out to their coworkers, their friends, and anyone in the family. I didn't edit myself because I didn't feel the need. I was out loud in their daily life. I no longer played the game of just not talking about it, and that was a bigger problem than my sister's drug addiction and child abuse.

Their shame and homophobia of having a queer son was the root of the backlash. I'm sure it stung like hell that out of all the people who could have stepped up, it was the queer who finally did something.

My biological family is riddled with secrets. One of the many quotes I learned to be true while I was working with addicts in my professional career was "You are only as sick as your secrets." While I do not subscribe to every notion presented in AA/NA, I do believe strongly in helping people and supporting them in working steps to identify character flaws and dysfunction in relationships. If it weren't for the fact that my family's dysfunction is seamless, some of them could have benefited from therapy of some sort. But when the family as a whole all play the same game, I will never win and I will never change it so I was forced to walk away from it. It was my only choice.

My family reacts like a colony of ants. They act as a collective. If an intruder enters, they attack. It became clear to me that not only could I not change that, but their inability to accept me was not a reflection of my self-worth. It took many years of on-and-off therapy for me to be able to say that last sentence. I still find it odd how the bad things we think about ourselves are so much easier to believe.

In the midst of this two-year battle, I was disillusioned and exhausted. My family's relentless push to keep up the harassment wasn't dying down. If anything, it was getting worse. Children's services and the court system had decided to return custody to my sister despite not having completed drug treatment and despite lack of proof of domestic violence counseling. I believe one of the many insane statements that the magistrate accepted from their attorney was "Well, he said he completed treatment but lost the certificate, so isn't that enough?"

I was fighting an uphill battle that I wasn't going to win. The longer this went on, the more my oldest niece suffered as she also became the target of their hate since she was the one who got out. Both she and I were the sole targets. I knew in my heart that she would return to their circle. It was all she knew after all. The longer I fought, the harder I was making it for her to reintegrate back into that dysfunction, which she would inevitably do. Although I got the occasional "thank you for all you've done" from my niece, the words were hollow, when in the end she went back to them and made zero effort to have any connection with me. I fought with everything I had to give her a home, protection, and sacrificed every last bit of peace and sanity I had left. I even lost my home to foreclosure due to insurmountable legal fees, all for absolutely nothing.

My sister had once again spent the better part of two years, not getting help or repairing a damaged relationship, but screaming loud enough, shouting gibberish allegations, and stomping her feet till she got what she wanted, creating deeper and more intense emotional trauma along the way to anyone who loved her. She put more energy into harassing the queer than it would have taken to get clean and sober. Because much of my extended family are either drug addicts, mentally ill or enablers of drug addicts, relationships imploded during those two years and more emotional damage was done that will never be repaired. Connections with random aunts, uncles and cousins fell away like dried shriveled flower petals, not worth saving.

In the end the kids weren't protected, and my family had become a civil war that had no end. I use the terms 'mentally ill' and drug addict' completely void of judgement. I state them merely as fact and all the reality attached to that fact.

I had come back to Ohio for my own reasons. I had tried to reconnect with my family, be a part of them, and try to help, to coexist. In the past two years I had watched my life devolve into utter chaos right along with theirs.

After two years of bitter attacks from my family, dealing with children's services' gross ineptness and the utter absurdity of the juvenile court system, I was tattered. The wind died down. Like a shredded flag after a storm, I could no longer fly.

Some years later I learned that children's service agencies get funding at the end of the year from the state for all the families they can categorize as reunified. For many agencies who operate in the red, reunification becomes much more important than child welfare.

Chapter Twenty-Four
Resolution

I often wondered why I felt instantly reduced to the mindset of a nervous teenager when I was with my parents and why I always felt the need to impress them, despite knowing the strength of my character.

In my search for peace and understanding, I've come to realize many things. My parents often refused to respect me as an adult, as an autonomous individual, because doing that would require them to acknowledge the harm they inflicted. They would have to own it.

This refusal stems from a deep-rooted psychological defense mechanism—denial. To respect me as an independent person with valid emotions, choices, and boundaries would mean confronting their own past actions. It would mean admitting that they were not just imperfect parents but, at times, willfully harmful ones.

Many abusive parents cannot or will not face this truth, as it threatens their self-image and forces them to reckon with guilt, shame, and accountability they are unwilling to bear.

Parents often engage in gaslighting behavior when confronted with these truths.

I've seen so many reflections of myself and my sister in the work I've done, understanding abusive parents and their relationships with their adult children.

Instead of facing these difficult emotions, they continue to treat their adult children as if they are still powerless, naive, and in need of control. They may infantilize them, dismiss their perspectives, or use manipulation to maintain dominance. This dynamic serves their need for control and reinforces their denial. If their child is still "just a kid who doesn't understand how the world works," then they, as parents, are still in a position of authority, absolved from past mistakes. I've seen this suppression play out with my sister her entire adult life.

This fuels an ongoing cycle of invalidation and emotional suppression, often leaving the child feeling small, unheard, and trapped in an emotional time warp where they are forever the vulnerable child seeking validation from an unyielding parent.

This experience is disorienting and is, by design, meant to make the adult child feel crazy.

I had built a successful life, developed emotional intelligence, and formed meaningful relationships, yet in the presence of my parents, I felt reduced to an insecure, confused version of myself. This regression happened because my parents refused to acknowledge my growth and instead continued to impose the old dynamics of control, criticism, or emotional neglect. I was always left feeling stuck between who I had become and who I was forced to be in my parents' presence.

This struggle is exacerbated by the societal expectation that family bonds should be preserved at all costs.

The phrases, "I am your mother!" And "You'll be sorry when I'm dead!" still ring in my ears. In reflection, I also see that these phrases always came on the heels of my parents avoiding responsibility for something, every time.

I've heard the following phrase often in my life: "Blood is thicker than water" This phrase is often interpreted to mean that family bonds are stronger than friendships or other relationships. However, some scholars believe this is a misinterpretation of a possibly older expression, "The blood of the covenant is thicker than the water of the womb."

While there is some scholarly disagreement over which version is older, the modern meaning that family is more important than friendship is almost always brought up to defend and justify toxic relationships with abusive family members. The words themselves are weapons to punish adult children for setting boundaries.

Many people who have never experienced this dynamic fail to understand the depth of harm caused by an abusive parent's refusal to acknowledge their child's adulthood. The adult child is often pressured to maintain the relationship despite the ongoing emotional damage. This pressure reinforces the painful reality that their pain may never be acknowledged, forcing them to navigate the complex landscape of maintaining boundaries while struggling with a lingering desire for parental validation.

Healing from this dynamic requires a conscious effort to break free from the emotional hold of the past. It's my main purpose for writing this book. Many adult children find solace in therapy, support groups, and chosen families who respect and affirm their autonomy. Establishing boundaries becomes essential—limiting contact, demanding respectful interactions, or, in some cases, choosing estrangement, as I did. The key to healing has been recognizing that my worth and maturity are not dependent on my parents' acknowledgment.

For me, true growth comes from self-validation, embracing the reality of my experiences, and building a life where I am seen, respected, and loved for who I truly am, not who my parents think I should have been.

Chapter Twenty-Five
Moving Forward

Amid all the family conflict I've described, I married my partner, Rowan. In a search for some queer culture, I had joined the Columbus Gay Men's Chorus to meet new friends. I loved performing, and given how utterly gut-wrenching the past few years had been, I had few opportunities aside from the occasional karaoke outing.

I had come back from California and within only a couple of years, had gotten mixed up in my sister's custody hell, and in all that time, I really hadn't made any time to build any kind of support system. I had few friends, which to me was painful because I have always identified as an extrovert. It became much more visible after I walked away from my bio family. The noise of profound family dysfunction had died down not because anything had changed but because I had walked away. I realized I didn't have much else in my life.

If you identify as a member of the queer community, you know better than most, that we often are forced to create our own families. We do it out of necessity. Personally, I felt so sad that I had to do it at all. I had lost so much and it would be many years before that lost the sting it had at the time. In retrospect, I wish I had the foresight to build a better support system for myself before I had to blow up that bridge between me and my folks.

I was so engulfed in the muck of it all that it snuck up on me till the day I realized I could no longer have these people in my life no matter how much pain that brought, and it did; more than I can ever explain.

The situation with my family had gotten so hostile I no longer felt physically safe. Any relationships I had with cousins or extended family had been strained by the family drama. I had no one. I also had no reason to stay in that town a minute longer. All that energy of hope and effort to be close to family, to not adopt children until I was close to them so my kids would have a support system, all of it was for nothing.

I cut off all contact with my biological family. I had told them throughout the years of harassment, "keep fucking with me and I'll leave and I won't tell anyone where I'm going."

That's exactly what I did. I've been gone for over 10 years. I live 3 hours away, and I've never heard from any of them. It may sound odd after all the shit I tolerated but I like to believe that they think of me, that maybe they google me to see how I'm doing. I like to think that somewhere in the deepest parts of their hearts, they miss me, especially my mom. I want to believe that she's trapped in a life she created, that she's scared to death to leave her husband, that she regrets choosing a simple-minded man with rage issues over her own children. I want to believe that. I want to believe that she regrets her blind loyalty. I want to believe she misses me. I want to believe that she grieves losing a second son.

You could say this wish list is selfish. I suppose it is. I don't wish emotional suffering on anyone, even them.

Here's the clincher though: The alternative to the hope that any of them love and miss me is the possibility that my parents, all four of them, are so deep in their religious delusions and toxic dysfunctional patterns that they have created a watertight narrative that drowned out any version of truth a long time ago. So what's worse? The idea that my family hates me or the idea that the estrangement is a tragedy born of such severe toxicity that even love couldn't prevent it.

I grieve people who aren't dead. I also grieve people who never existed.

It's weird. I think the assumption of course is that we learn how to parent and build our own families by using our own childhood experiences as a template for normality. We fill in the blanks. For me, a starting point has been to give my kids what I didn't have: understanding, safety, freedom and autonomy.

It's been hard in their absence for many reasons. I mean, yes, I am relieved, and yes, I am exponentially better off without the abuse and dysfunction, and I absolutely have a more functional and fulfilled life. This is all true. It's hard because, despite having made a healthy functional choice for myself and my family, I grieve who they should have been.

My father's name was Donald Marlow. I was named after him. When my husband and I got married, I not only took my husband's last name, but I also changed my first name to Daniel. My father was always quick to take credit for my life achievements in public, but was equally quick to judge and ridicule who I was as a person behind closed doors. Sharing a name with him carried with it a toxic connection that no longer served me.

I took no pride in the name Marlow. My last name had become synonymous with ignorance, criminal records, drug use, and a general dysfunctional toxicity to which I simply had no connection. My husband, I, and our children are all Keltys. We give ourselves permission to define what that name means.

I currently operate a private practice where I specialize in ecotherapy.

I teach people to find peace in nature, much like I did with that fox in the woods when I was a boy.

I also have a consulting program where I teach people in the LGBTQ community how to heal from toxic family wounds.

While my path through this trauma and subsequent healing has been unpredictable, I think the one thing that surprised me the most is how isolated I had become. It hasn't been a conscious choice, but I had some maladaptive coping strategies. One of those has been, in the hyper vigilance of my healing, I had zero tolerance for human error in my friendships. While my standards for new friends in my life have become high, they have also, in some cases, become unattainable.

In the past few years, when someone let me down or disappointed me in some way, I shut them out. I burned the bridge and walked away. I did it often with folks here in Zanesville because their culture reminded me so much of my birth family. It has been very triggering.

Initially, this felt like I was finally setting some firm boundaries. My inner dialogue went something like this: "I walked away from my own parents! Why the fuck should I tolerate anything from you?"

On the surface, this thought had a hint of healthy coping, but the reality has been that it's also left me quite lonely. I had to learn to tolerate human error again. It was primarily what inspired my consulting program. I found many sources to help me set limits, but far fewer that taught me how to trust people again. It has been a rebirth of sorts. I know I have hurt the feelings of some well-intended people here locally. While I can't undo that, I can learn from it.

I still find it amazing what we tolerate from our families of origin. No longer will I tolerate bad behavior, especially bad behavior that would harm my children. Genetics have nothing to do with my definition of family. Family are the people who celebrate you. Family is who supports you and loves you because of who you are, not despite who you are.

Biological family is where we come from. Armistead Maupin, author of "Tales of the City" coined the phrase 'logical family.' That's the family we get to choose.

I think I'm ready to live life instead of just surviving it. I am stepping back into a new rhythm with this still flawed, yet wiser version of myself. I need to learn how to make friends again. I need to trust people again. More than that though, I need to trust me.

Chapter Twenty-Six
My Career

I don't recall ever having a career goal to be a psychotherapist or even work in the field of psychology. I didn't feel drawn to it so much as it was simply a part of who I've always been. I need to understand things. I believe words have power and I believe that it matters how you treat people and how you make them feel. These core values led me to finding myself in grad school.

My career in mental health began long before grad school and in fact before my undergrad. The conception of my career in mental health took place in San Francisco. I worked at a halfway house designed for populations who had been in locked psych wards for 10 years or more. Much of the government funding had been cut to treat this population, so these alternative transitional housing nonprofits started sprouting up showing all over the bay area.

My first house was for people still experiencing active delusions and psychosis. My job was to teach them how to do things like wash the dishes, make their bed, prepare a simple meal, etc. The reality was more like running around the two-story Victorian house in Pacific Heights, constantly putting out emotional fires created by mental illness. It was convincing clients to attend support groups even though they possibly thought there was a dragon in the hallway.

My first client assigned to me was a young woman whose seemingly fixed pupil gaze was in stark contrast to her widely expressive smiles. The people I worked with were rarely dangerous, but could easily solicit a creepy vibe simply by their lack of social norms, tremors caused by medication side effects and, of course the delusional content in their behavior. It was often visually unsettling. It always makes me sad when I think about the fact that at some point, these people were someone's little baby girl or someone's new baby boy, then they ended up in that halfway house. Hallowed expressions trapped in their own minds.

That first part-time fill in position taught me more about people suffering from psychosis more than anything I have experienced in career. I stuck with it and eventually got a permanent counseling position.

I vividly remember sitting in the outdoor smoking area during one of my overnight shifts, watching a disheveled old woman, slumped over, dressed in mix-matched layers of clothing, chain-smoking her Marlboro lights with a methodical Intentionality. I remember her yellow, tar-stained hands and fingers trembling as she drew each cigarette to her overly pursed lips. Her true identity had long ago been consumed her delusions, which were like little tiny rats scurrying about in her brain. She could never quiet them.

I saw human suffering on a visceral level. I think every mental health clinician should do a round in the trenches, so to speak. It was a great lesson in the resilience of the human spirit.

In the years that followed, I held similar positions in various nonprofit organizations as a case manager and counselor. In the last few years I spent in San Francisco I was the housing case manager for the city and county of San Francisco under Proposition 36. This was a proposition that allowed first-time offenders who had been arrested for a nonviolent drug or alcohol offence to serve their time in rehab instead of jail. Many of these same folks were homeless and in need of housing. The city owned three hotels in the Tenderloin district of San Francisco. The geographic irony is that the Tenderloin, or 'the TL' as locals call it, was also the best place to score any drug you wanted. It was also a place where you did not venture out after dark. Likely the worst place in the world for someone seeking recovery. On a warm summer day the breeze often carried the stench of urine from the tiny alleys tucked between adjacent buildings. The drug deals were not confined to these tucked-away places. They were out in the open on the front door steps of run down buildings. The darker more secluded little corners of the TL was often where people lost their battles with addiction.

I managed three different hotels in that neighborhood. I had the misfortune of discovering more than one dead body in that job. Addiction is a son of a bitch and does not discriminate. The underbelly of this reality is often more visible in poverty-stricken communities, not because poor people use more drugs, but because they frequently lack the resources to get out. The Tenderloin was no exception.

I like to think that with each step in my career, I've become a bit more well-rounded along the way. The stepping stones I created in California have been crucial to where I am now.

When I left Ohio originally, I was a 19-year-old kid with no work experience. I returned as a 38-year-old version of myself, equipped with a bachelor's degree, a year of grad school, and a wealth of professional experience. I had two noteworthy positions upon moving back to Ohio.

The first was one you couldn't pay enough to ever do again: a case worker for child protective services (CPS) in Montgomery County. I did it for two years. I saw countless families suffering from multi-generational trauma, addiction, lack of education, and mental illness. I also quickly learned that CPS has no real ability or desire to protect children at all. The internal corruption in the agency's ineptness was no less than the dysfunction experienced by families in the community who desperately need their services. One fueled the other and vice versa. It was a cyclical bureaucracy of dysfunction that does no more to protect children than fleas protect dogs. A sometimes controversial ideology, but it's a hill I'll die on.

The other was my first job out of grad school at Hospice of Dayton. I had worked two hospice internships in grad school, so I thought I knew a bit about what I was signing up for.

Dying is something we are all going to do. It doesn't matter how much money you have in the bank or what degree you have hanging on your wall. We all die. The hard part is that we don't talk about it and often spend our entire lives fearing it.

One of my passions is how children experience grief in regard to the loss of a loved one. It was work that felt so organic to me. I've helped educate patients and families about the dying process and talked with them about what to expect. I've sat with people and held their hands as they've died. I've watched their stillness after the last breath leaves their body.

After all these years, I still struggle with finding appropriate words to describe that moment. There's something profound about watching someone's chest rise and fall, waiting for their death, and then seeing their chest not rise again. It's so quiet and uneventful. I found that no matter how many times I experienced that, I was keenly aware and grateful for the first breath I took in that same room, that they were not able to take. It's the most humbling feeling.

People often ask, "How can you do that? I could never do that."

My reply has always been, "It's simply an honor to be present. It's (dying) something we are all going to do. It's an honor just to be present with people on the worst day of their lives."

That's all you have to do, just be present and hold compassionate space. It's more often as powerful as any words, in my opinion, that we can offer in that moment. Just be present and listen.

My job as a grief therapist was to provide comfort in several capacities. Sometimes I provided emotional support to the person who was dying, and sometimes I supported their families before, during, and after the death. I could write an entire book on this experience alone. It was life-changing, and I learned more in those few years about what life is about than I could have ever imagined.

I have numerous stories I could share about meaningful deaths I have experienced. One that sticks out in my mind was one of the first deaths I ever experienced. He was a man in his 60s dying of cancer. Unlike most cancer patients near the end of life, he was awake and alert. Typically, people who die from different kinds of cancer will often be unconscious for several days leading up to their deaths. This gentleman was fully awake alone in his room.

Walking past the nurses' station, I often checked their records to see who I should check in on. I hate for anyone to die alone, and when I learned that he showed several medical signs of end-of-life, I made him a priority for my rounds.

His door was open. I peeked my head into the doorway as I gently knocked on the door as I entered the room. He had no visitors or family present.

I introduced myself and said, "I noticed you were alone in here and I just wanted to know if you'd like some company."

He tilted his head and gave me a smirk, then said, "You're kinda weird, aren't you?"

The surprise on my face made him smile more. I remember muttering as I returned his smirk, "Well, I guess so, yeah. What makes you say that?"

His smile had a warmth to it. He looked so content as he spoke again: "You can come in, but I'm not alone, son. There are all kinds of people in this room."

He gazed around the room with that same warm smile and died peacefully minutes later.

My hospice career was filled with so many poignant moments like this. I grew as a human, and I'll always be grateful for that experience. I firmly believe that our life experiences change us. Helping professionals are particularly susceptible to burnout for this very reason.

Although it was not from conscience strategizing, I realized that I would spend no more than 2-3 years at any given job, then I'd move on to something else. Maybe it was my ADHD. I don't know. I just seemed to realize at the 2-3 year mark that I needed something else or that there was a certain aspect of the job to which I felt ill-matched. There were parts of my work that fed my soul. There were also parts of my work that fed on me, leaving me feeling like Swiss cheese. I had to find balance.

I had spent a few years working with the homeless, then a few years in addiction, then a few working with children and families, a few years in community mental health and lastly with bereavement populations. All this experience made me a well-rounded clinician, but I still didn't know where I wanted to be.

Chapter Twenty-Seven
Wild Ohio

When I decided I could no longer have my family in my life. My urgency looked spontaneous. The reality was that it had taken many years for that sentiment to build up till it choked me, so we packed up and left just like I kept warning them I would. I walked away from every last one of them without formality and without explanation. I just left. I still sometimes wonder how that was received. I'll never know. The leaving was much more important than where I was headed. It could have been anywhere.

As I felt the tension and pressure building, Rowan and I had been online looking at farmland for several months. I was limited to Ohio only because my professional license had me on a state-wide tether.

We bought a 50-acre farm just outside of Zanesville in a little town called Roseville. The in-town part of Roseville was simply a straight, narrow stretch of road populated with churches, hardware stores, and private residences. The main gas station in town was also a small convenience store where people gathered on their quads, side-by-sides, or lawn mowers. Scratch-off lottery tickets and Mountain Dew were staples for most folks.

It was common to find families living in doublewide trailers flying Confederate flags. To be fair, there were also just as many nice, cute, well-kept homes sitting on corner lots with fenced yards. These houses also often flew Confederate flags.

Interestingly, though, as I've mentioned, we rarely experienced any overt racism. People clearly had what I perceived to be their ignorant belief systems, but none of it caused me any harm personally. There were swirls of populations consisting of first and second generations of Appalachia. Anyone not from Roseville, were often from places like West Virginia and Kentucky. When I think about the people of Roseville, I think: poor education, poverty, muti-generational trauma, and religion; along with all the dysfunction that comes with each of those categories. That is Roseville, Ohio.

Just past the bridge leaving town, there was a winding road to the left. This narrow road circled and climbed what felt like a mountain. This area is famous for hills like that. It was largely due to the fact that millions of years ago, the glaciers from the ice age never reached this part of what is now Ohio, leaving it rugged and heavily eroded. These hills and hair pin curves of most roads made driving more treacherous in the best of conditions.

At the top of this hill, the land flattened out a bit and held pockets of wooded areas and farm houses. Most of our property was covered in dense undergrowth and few walking paths. It was a young, wooded area due to the town's history of fracking and strip mining. Much of the land was thick with thorns and dense overgrown weeds. To some it may have looked desolate. To me, it was peace and tranquility. I needed a quiet place.

The old farmhouse was a white two-story structure with a small stone patio for outdoor fires and a wooden deck that had been added in recent years. The interior had been made over with bare bones and a minimum investment. Cheap peel-and-stick flooring covered most of the floors.

The house had a bright red metal roof that set it apart from the scattered homes on that curvy road. Just behind the house, there was a matching shed. The siding was worn by the wind over the years. Poorly insulated and built on a slab, this house was a skeleton of what I hoped it could be someday and certainly what it once was.

We definitely went into that situation with willful blindness. For me, all I cared about was that we were now 3 hours away from my birth family, and I could finally experience some self-created distance between myself and them. That's what this move was all about for me. I desperately needed to find a safe place to lick my wounds, and if that happened to be in a dilapidated old farmhouse sitting on 50 acres of my own, land, all the better. The only thing I think I would change if I could go back was that I would not have lied when the seller asked me if I knew what a dry well was and if I was okay with a house with a dry well.

I just heard the word well and thought, "Ok well there is no water connected to the town, so the house has a well, ok, cool."

A dry well is another term for a cistern, so we had to haul water ourselves from town or find someone to deliver it for us. It was impossible to gauge how much water was in the well at any given time, and we ran out of water several times, which caused constant hardship. I've never felt more like Laura Ingles Wilder than living in Roseville, Ohio.

Back in the 70s Roseville was the pottery hub for this part of Ohio due to the high amount of clay deposits in the ground. Today, Roseville is still recognized for its pottery heritage, with collectors seeking out pieces from its golden era of ceramic production. The clay content is not good news for gardening enthusiasts though.

I found myself spending more and more time outside among the trees. The solitude of being outside at night whispered a feeling of spirituality and healing. It was a rough place to be. It was untamed and took a great deal of effort to navigate the wooded areas. Alone with my thoughts, I often found myself wandering through the woods, trying to find myself. It was sometimes a dangerous place to be.

The wildlife in Roseville was abundant. Wild turkeys, deer, coyotes, and bobcats all made their home with ours. The coyotes' cries at night gave me chills, not out of fear but rather a healthy respect for their presence.

Our house sat at the uppermost crest of the hill, so most of our pastures dipped off into sloping hills, creating a valley on one side of the property. I remember one night, in particular, I went outside to take the trash out. Walking across the patio I often allowed my eyes to scan the tree line down in the valley much like you look at the guy next to you at a red light. I looked over and gasped!

At the edge of the woods, there were probably a couple of dozen glowing yellow eyes staring back at me! I could see some movement. They wouldn't come out of the woods, but the glowing eyes would shift and reappear as the pack paced back and forth. Their cries and howls sounded like a yearning.

We had some livestock during our time at the farm, like goats and rabbits. Not that coyotes needed a reason, but our farm must have enticed them. Oddly enough, though, they never gave us any trouble. They were just constantly reminding us that they were there first. The coyotes didn't really scare me. If anything gave me the creeps, it was the black snakes so huge and long, we often saw them climbing the trees in the spring to eat baby birds. We saw one once that I swear had to be close to six feet long. We had chickens, so the snakes were frequent visitors.

I had never in my life experienced having so much space. I could easily have gotten lost on my own property. The woods surrounded our little house and gave a nice refuge from the outside world. I felt at peace, but I was also quite lonely. Aside from the occasional liberal client, I really didn't have much social contact with other people. I began to rely on animals for much of my social needs, not consciously, but I began to do more animal rehab/rescue. I began to realize I needed them as much as they needed me.

It was definitely a coping strategy for me.

Over the few years we lived there, we acquired horses, mini horses, tame white-tailed deer, pigs, peacocks, ducks, a couple of coyotes and foxes in need of rehab, as well as raccoons and opossums. They all called our home theirs.

Out in the country, I had become known as "the animal guy." Subsequently, I became a magnet for anyone who knew anyone who had a litter of baby raccoons they needed help with. It was not uncommon for a litter of squirrels or kittens to show up on my front doorstep.

I still chuckle when I recall the day I came inside from caring for the horses as I did daily. I was casually holding an injured red cardinal in my hand. Rowan bursts out in laughter:

"How do you do that!? Who the fuck are you?, Snow White.?!"

We both laughed. He was right, though. I didn't have to go looking for any of them. They all seemed to find me.

I know at some point Rowan became annoyed, or rather didn't understand my caring for animals in need. I remember driving down our dark road one night on my way to the grocery store. I heard that distinct thump thump that told me I had hit something that only a moment prior was trying to scurry across the road.

I cringed and let out a grunt when I realized I had hit an opossum. I immediately pulled over to the side of the road and put the car in park.

Rowan instantly rolled his eyes as he said sharply, "What are you doing??"

He wasn't any less annoyed when I told him, "It's birthing season, that opossum might be carrying babies in her pouch!"

Moments later, much to the chagrin of my supportive husband, I got back into the car with 10 little fleshy squeaky bundles of joy cradled in the excess of my baggy shirt. I was the one who killed her. I had to try. I couldn't just leave them there to die on the side of the road.

I trusted animals more than people, including the pack of coyotes that shared our property with us. My soul began to find peace in caring for all of them. With each eye dropper full of milk and each heating pad, I realized I was not just helping them. I was also healing tiny pieces of myself.

Chapter Twenty-Eight
Deer Farming

White tailed deer hunting in Ohio is a primal part of Apalachin culture. The deer in Roseville were plentiful during breeding season. They could also actually be a significant hazard as the bucks (males) come out of the deep woods to find mates. During this time, known as the rut, which coincides with hunting season, the deer are numerous and pay no attention to cars or traffic, as evidenced by the many deer lying dead on the shoulder of the roads.

In terms of hunting, for men, killing a deer is a rite of passage. It is embedded in their gender expectations. The preferred prize, of course, was the male deer with antlers. The more points the antlers boasted, the older and more dominant the deer.

Hunters of all ages hike the woods stalking and ambushing deer every hunting season. It's highly regulated and carries stiff penalties for poachers or undocumented hunters. There are even specific time frames distinguishing whether firearms or bows can be used. The focus of law enforcement, ODNR, is to promote wildlife conservation through regulated population control. I could never in a million years do it, but I understand the necessity.

Deer are large, prolific animals that now have no natural predators since the eradication of wolves and large cats. Much of that is the fault of humans, so now we must rebalance the ecosystem through hunting. I do understand and respect the process, but I will never comprehend people who seemingly enjoy killing things and hanging dead animal heads in their den. I think it's a custom that has been popularly normalized within many cultures, but I still find it disturbing.

Some of the more privileged can experience a guaranteed kill if they hunt on hunting preserves. Deer raised on hunting farms have been born in captivity and live in fenced-in areas where they are shot and killed, unable to escape. It's a controlled DNA pool, so the farmers breed for the largest racks possible, then charge hunters a premium cost to hunt there. Not only are tame animals bred and killed for human entertainment, but it also did nothing to help control the wild population.

The farmers also sell the lucrative deer semen to other farmers from the most sought-after bucks. The entire industry is quite expansive.

White-tailed deer farming in Ohio began gaining popularity in the 1990s and early 2000s, driven by increased demand for deer-related industries such as hunting preserves, venison production, and antler sales.

Ohio is now one of the leading states for captive deer farming, with hundreds of licensed operations. The industry remains somewhat controversial due to concerns over disease transmission (like Chronic Wasting Disease), ethical hunting debates, and ecological impact.

Behind the fences of Ohio's deer farms, wild hearts are bred for profit, their grace reduced to a commodity. These creatures, born to roam the whispering woods and dance with the changing seasons, are instead confined—engineered for antlers, for trophies, for a moment of human vanity. Their dignity is traded for sport, their fate sealed before they ever taste true freedom. To mold life for gain, to shape beauty only to take it away, is to deny the sacred wildness that pulses through all living things. A creature that should flee with the wind should never be raised to fall by design.

It's simply a horrible industry. In addition, I was horrified to learn that many farmers would actually euthanise fawns if there was a surplus of females. I also learned that with a captive deer permit purchased from ODNR, which is not easy to qualify for, you could purchase some of these fawns that would otherwise be put down.

We acquired several fawns over the years. Sometimes, the farmers even offered them for free. I had very mixed feelings about it, but I also knew that for the individuals we took in, it was life-saving. I soon became known as a contact for farmers looking to get rid of surplus fawns.

We raised bottle-fed deer, who subsequently became extraordinarily tame and social. They would even come running up to us when we called for them. It was magical. Complete strangers sometimes pulled into the driveway just to see the deer. I had just started seeing clients one-on-one on the farm. Clients loved spending their therapy sessions out in the pasture feeding deer.

ODNR requires 8' tall fences so it was a huge expense to fence in a pasture for the deer. We also had to deal with surprise inspections from ODNR when they showed up randomly to measure the fences or to make sure that the deer we had all wore ear tags to prove we didn't kidnap them from the wild. This was an important distinction because these deer were rescued much like you rescue a dog from a kill shelter. These deer got to have a life free of being corn fed then shot for sport.

Although I was able get a rehab permit that allowed me to house several different kinds of wildlife, it is highly illegal to rehab or keep wild deer. For this reason, having tame deer that would eat from your hand made me quite popular.

Fresh goat's milk is the closest thing to deer milk, so of course, we also got some dairy goats. The deer were so much fun to bottle feed. They have voracious appetites and could down a bottle of goat's milk in seconds!

When considering the behavior of just about any animal, if you truly understand that species, and understand its place in the ecosystem, its temperament, what it's capable of, their behavior and reactions become somewhat predictable when exposed to specific stimuli.

You can't do this with humans. Humans lie. Humans manipulate. Humans have agendas. They also have the propensity for all kinds of cruelty with little to no predictability.

I had been wounded so profoundly and so deeply by the people who were supposed to love me the most. That reality was settling more into my bones as a fundamental truth. It was an emotionally raw time for me. My parents' birthdays often still left me in tears. I struggled to be present for my own children during family holidays because I was consumed with the pain of the family I had lost. Despite the fact that I was the one who made the choice to leave that dysfunctional collective, I still gave myself permission to grieve it because, at some point, it was all I knew to be familiar.

I came to realize that my anger was swirled together with profound sadness, with themes of resentment that were becoming less and less about their choices and more about who they could not be for me.

Those years were filled with so much self-realization. I heard people around me talking about caring for their elderly parents as their life roles reversed. It made me sad that I'd never be able to experience that.

In my years at hospice, I had the honor to be present for families as they said their goodbyes to their loved ones. I knew I would not be able to be present for the same rituals in my own family. I imagine I was living in my own head. I felt tortured by the memories of the custody battle with my sister. I remembered the smirk on my mother's face as she looked me in the eye, sitting in the witness stand as she offered testimony against me. Her disdain. She mocked me openly to anyone who'd listen. The pain from these memories burned into me. It changed me. It haunted me.

There was something else I began to realize. I was grieving people and scenarios that were fictional. I had a lifetime of evidence that reminded me, screaming into my ear. These life rituals, these funerals, these births and weddings; they would not be family/ life events woven together with compassion and acceptance.

They would much more likely be stitched together with the same threads of verbal abuse, tradition, and obligation. I had to exercise caution not to idealize their memory.

Chapter Twenty-Nine
What I Think I Know

If you were to ask me if I believe in a god or what my thoughts on an afterlife are, my answer would vary greatly depending on when you ask me.

My faith in a higher power is something I have often been at odds with. I still had an awful taste in my mouth for Christianity because of my childhood and subsequently found myself categorically opposed to anything that looked like it.

Like many queer people, I had Christianity and religion weaponized against me for as long as I can remember. Not only had I picked apart the painfully obvious loopholes in the Bible for most of my life, because I'm a critical thinker, but I also sometimes wondered if the notion of an afterlife was nothing more than a narrative created by humans who were afraid to die.

I hold an undefined deep sense of spirituality. Interestingly, though, still feel that the word atheist is the best word to describe myself. I am completely ok being wrong about all of it. This is just where I sit today.

I don't tell anyone else what they should believe. That's none of my business. I don't even tell my kids what they should believe. I give them education, encouragement, and trust, and they come to their own conclusions that resonate with them. My one son identified as a Buddhist for a while, even though I consider myself an atheist. Collectively, our family is a little bit of everything, and that's ok. All I can tell you is what I believe and what has served me.

I don't have the conviction of an evangelical nor the soft-spoken wisdom of a shaman. I don't pretend to have any answers, but what I think I know is that we are supposed to learn something in our time here. I also think we are supposed to love and accept one another. I don't think it's supposed to be much more complicated than that. I think it's we who make it complicated with our laws, our fear, and our need for the security of organized religion. I believe our lives are supposed to give us learning opportunities so that we can grow and evolve. I also think that it sometimes takes stumbling several times over several lifetimes.

I think the only punishment or suffering we experience is a self-induced place of a lack of love and connection. Regardless of which part of the "pale blue dot" we call home, the task is the same: Learn, grow, and find love and connectedness. That's it.

Chapter Thirty
A New Beginning

In the many years since this story began, I've been married to my husband Rowan for 16 years. He is not perfect, and our relationship is not perfect, but he would stop time for me if he could. I have seen him grow and evolve when I needed his support the most. He was there when I was falling apart. He was there when I raged and has been present for me in ways many people would not have been. He and I are proud dad and papa to three children. We adopted two little boys who were 3 and 4 years old, respectively. They are now 18 and 19 years old. Our daughter was only a day old when she came into our lives. She is now 7 years old.

Every single day, I learn how to be a better dad. I understand that adult children do not owe their parents a relationship because there was food on the table, a roof over their heads, or they loved them. That's the bare minimum. That adult relationship is earned. It is earned by mutual respect and autonomy. I will always love certain people in my family, but I owe them nothing.

Loving them from a distance is only the first step. The most challenging part is holding the fact that love actually magnifies the burden of estrangement.

I hold tightly to this lesson as I watch my kids grow. Even now, as my sons are young adults, they don't owe me anything. The respect I get from them doesn't come from my demanding it. It comes from a seed I plant every time I show them respect and listen to how they feel. If they get angry with me, I don't personalize it. I validate it and try to understand it. Their emotions and experiences do not need my approval.

Jon

My son Jon, I believe, has been on this earth many times before. I see the old man's wisdom in his coy glances and his infectious keen humor. Always carrying the weight from the stigma of his educational IEP, I've often seen him feel so insecure and uncertain. He struggled to embrace his inherent intelligence frequently.

I see, in him, a reflection of how stupid I always felt as a child. I was utterly convinced that I was not smart. That belief always seemed to be reflected in what I found wrong with the world. If someone didn't want to be my friend, I assumed it was due to my own deficiency. I thought it was because I wasn't enough. Jon has always given me the feeling that he also sees himself in that description growing up. In fact, I didn't fully realize how I felt about myself as a child until I saw Jon act out his own version of it.

As he grew, I began to hear my own words come from his mouth as he comforted me in my healing. The same words I used in his childhood to comfort him about his perceived imperfections and faults, he began to use with me.

Many times he has told me "Dad, it's OK, you are doing the best you can."

Jon has grown into a young man whom I respect deeply. His depth of emotion and raw assertiveness leave me in awe.

He has exploded into this confident, vibrant young man, thirsty for knowledge, and is now attending the college of his dreams, making and designing video games.

Timothy

My son, Timothy, is Jon's biological brother and one year younger. He carries a heavy silence. He is quite comfortable with limited verbal conversation, especially if it's small talk or chit chat. When he speaks, he means it. He also possesses a tough masculine energy that is embraced by a bewitching charm that adults have noticed his entire life. He values his privacy deeply and struggles asking for help.

Timothy's brotherly competitiveness has sometimes prevented him from having as much fun as he could, but his success fuels him. Timothy has a drive that will shoot him beyond the stars if he can figure out how to harness it. He has a burning urge to succeed. He pours his energy into weightlifting and making himself as strong as possible.

His vibration is deeper than most of his peers, leaving him with few friends. In recent years, I have seen him pour his energy into his inner self and again, making himself as strong as possible...almost like he's compensating for something, for past chances not taken.

I once had a psychic medium tell me that he is my brother reincarnated. It is true that I consciously named him after my brother, Timothy.

Maybe I'm seeing a connection because I want to. I don't know. Maybe there is a spiritual connection that I am now privileged to care for his soul. Is it possible that my brother decided he couldn't stay with our family? Maybe he reincarnated when he knew I could care for him. I don't know. What I do know is that Timothy is the person I go to when I need grounding. He is his own foundation, and I can't wait to see what he builds.

Some of the most endearing moments of my life have been those where I can watch the boys' relationship evolve from a fierce competitive sibling rivalry to an equal curiosity of who they both are becoming from their own perspectives.

Lily

Our male-dominated family has had its normal ebbs and flows. Then, when I turned 50, our daughter Lily made a surprise appearance in our lives. I had secretly yearned for a daughter for years. There was something about that female energy that was so intoxicating to me. I rarely verbalized it and had put that dream to rest long ago.

Through an unexpected turn of events, we were contacted by our local foster care agency about a baby girl abandoned at the hospital after her birth. Not given a name, just left. We later changed this narrative to a story of finding her at "the baby store." We explained to her how elated we were to find her after dreaming about her for years before she even existed. We explained that her birth mommy just didn't know how to keep her safe, but that she loved her enough to make sure she found a loving family, so she placed her at the baby store in the hospital so Daddy and Papa could come pick her up, and we did.

Biological relatives would surface later in opposition, but this was short-lived. For a time, she was a nameless infant. We picked her up from the maternity ward, gave her the name Lily, and later legally adopted her.

Although unexpected, Lily has proven to be a force, an enormous gust of wind that we didn't even know we needed. She awakened all my horrible dad jokes, much to the chagrin of my now teenage sons. She wears her heart on the outside and subsequently craves acceptance. She is fully aware of her gender difference and the transfixion we have all experienced, being wrapped around her little fingers.

We have always offered Lily toys like Lincoln logs, marbles, and matchbox cars. Equally, she has had access to the more predictable glittery pink princess toys. She has adamantly and forcefully chosen the latter consistently. She's a loud and rough-playing princess who loves her jewelry while playing in the mud.

Lily is my biggest weakness and has completely and totally captured my heart. Her love is like something I have never known. She has awakened something in me that I didn't even know existed.

As the boys are nearing their adulthood, she has been the wind that has rekindled the hot ashes back to a flame. These three souls are my world, and looking after them has been the greatest privilege of my life.

As an adult, I have lived enough life to understand what's at stake. Wisdom brings caution, but it doesn't mean my courage has disappeared. It just got quieter, waiting for me to remember it. That's the magic of a relationship like I have with my kids— it's not just parent to child. It's legacy to legacy. I've raised two brave young men, and in doing so, I've rediscovered the brave man I still am.

Although I don't believe in a god, I do believe there is something after all of this. One of my passions is researching near-death experiences. I have followed the work of different people like Louisa Peck, a friend, a published author, and a writing coach.

Through her stories of her own near-death experience, she talks about how we choose the lives we have and how we are supposed to learn something from them.

Christian Sunberg, also a renowned and highly respected author within spiritual communities, suggests that miscarriages, for example, can be the result of a soul changing its mind to incarnate, as was his experience.

Just recently, as I was driving my son, Jon, back to college after a weekend visit, I thought of something. I'd love to do some research on this topic, though I have no idea how I'd go about it. The souls of adopted children, children who knew they wouldn't stay with their birth mothers... If we embrace the concept that we choose who we are born to, then my children, whom I adopted, must have had some insight that they'd end up with me, or if not, then they were aware the women they were born to would not care for them.

Either way, it really makes me wonder about the correlation between their souls being brave enough to incarnate into such a turbulent beginning, and then here I am grieving the loss of my parents, whom I had for most of my life. I had the privilege of navigating that loss as an adult with my frontal lobe intact, allowing me to reason and understand for the most part. My children were not afforded that luxury.

Maybe these souls and I were meant to share the painful journey of the loss of birth parents. Maybe they knew I'd need their support, that I needed a family as much as they did. Maybe they knew that I'd also need to be reminded of the humility that I am not alone in losing my parents, and of course, in that, in all our brokenness and incompleteness, together has made us quite complete and whole after all.

The souls of adopted children fascinate me. I think perhaps they are the bravest of us all.

The Beat Goes On

This book was a painful, beautiful process. My career as a therapist has certainly helped me understand my own process and given me the tools I needed to care for myself as I worked. I have been working as a therapist and in some capacity in social services for over 20 years. My career has taken me to some interesting places and shown me some unflattering reflections of myself. Following my own moral compass has helped me not get lost in all of it. In my line of work, burnout is common and sometimes difficult to avoid. I am no exception to that trend. I have drastically reduced my caseload in my therapy practice and now only see a few clients. I have redirected the majority of my energy into an unexpected endeavor.

When I completed this book, I was exhausted. I had to relive so much in order to capture and share these parts of my life with you. Throughout the process, I often found myself reflecting on just how soul-crushing it felt during the estrangement process and the years that followed. I realized how much I suffered. I also realized something else: My community had no resources to help me navigate my specific problem. I tried therapy, but couldn't find the right connection. All kinds of queer people experience estrangement. Their culture and their circumstances are all unique to each person. Despite this, I still felt like there were enough commonalities in this population to justify creating something new. So, as I experienced somewhat of a death in my desire to do therapy, I also experienced the birth of my life consulting program specifically for queer people dealing with estrangement.

People trying to survive this kind of loss often need more than a diagnosis. They need a soul connection. In my 10-week program, I work intimately with people navigating a path from estrangement to resilience. I also offer a year-long program for people who want a deeper exploration of their issues, or maybe they just need more ongoing support. This is one of my favorite parts of the consulting process, where I get to meet people outside the DSM-IV and connect in a much more personal way. I can't tell you what it would have meant to me if I had someone to hold my hand while I put pieces of myself back together after the loss of my family. So, in that vein, I provide for others what I didn't have. You can find more information about my services at

www.danielkelty.com

My husband has been my rock. His patience, endless support and super hero editing skills have been an essential part of my success. I could not have done this without him.

About the Author

Daniel was born in Dayton, Ohio. He is also a wartime decorated veteran from the Navy. Daniel holds a bachelor's degree in psychology, a master's degree in social work, and a certification in ecotherapy. He is a licensed mental health professional who operates a private practice called Wild Ohio Therapy Farm LLC.

Daniel also provides life coaching aimed at issues of estrangement and resilience. He is passionate about art and has a mosaic/stained glass business called Broken Dreams LLC. He and his husband have been married for 16 years and they have three children. Daniel and his family reside in Ohio but are seeking residency in Costa Rica. Daniel's coaching services are available online internationally.

www.ingramcontent.com/pod-product-compliance
Lightning Source LLC
Chambersburg PA
CBHW071742120626

46550CB00002B/624

9798999027504